Nourish Nova Scotia

PRESENTS

WHAT'S FOR LUNCH?

Nova Scotia Recipes to Cook and Enjoy Together

With illustrations by Emma FitzGerald
Designed by Denise Postma

Nourish Nova Scotia

NOVA SCOTIA

NIMBUS PUBLISHING LTD.
NIMBUS.CA

Nimbus Publishing Limited | 3660 Strawberry Hill Street, Halifax, NS, B3K 5A9 | (902) 455-4286 nimbus.ca

Printed and bound in Canada

NB1858

Co-authors: Jenny Osburn & Aimee Gasparetto | Editor: Hilary Briar | Design: Denise Postma | Photography: Lia Chin-Yet | Art: Emma FitzGerald

Library and Archives Canada Cataloguing in Publication

Title: What's for lunch? : Nova Scotia recipes to cook and enjoy together / with illustrations by Emma FitzGerald ; designed by Denise Postma. Other titles: What's for lunch? (2025) Names: FitzGerald, Emma, 1982- illustrator | Nourish Nova Scotia, issuing body. Description: At head of title: Nourish Nova Scotia presents.

Identifiers: Canadiana (print) 20250261375 | Canadiana (ebook) 20250261383 | ISBN 9781774715079 (softcover) | ISBN 9781774715086 (EPUB)

Subjects: LCSH: Luncheons—Nova Scotia. | LCSH: Lunchbox cooking—Nova Scotia. | LCSH: School children—Food—Nova Scotia. | LCSH: Luncheons—Nova Scotia—Anecdotes. | LCSH: Lunchbox cooking Nova Scotia—Anecdotes. | LCSH: School children—Food—Nova Scotia—Anecdotes. | LCGFT: Cookbooks. | LCGFT: Anecdotes. Classification: LCC TX735 .W43 2025 | DDC j641.5/309716—dc23

Canada

Canada Council for the Arts Conseil des arts du Canada

NOVA SCOTIA

Nimbus Publishing acknowledges the financial support for its publishing activities from the Government of Canada, the Canada Council for the Arts, and from the Province of Nova Scotia. We are pleased to work in partnership with the Province of Nova Scotia to develop and promote our creative industries for the benefit of all Nova Scotians.

Land Acknowledgment

This cookbook was created by Nourish Nova Scotia.

We acknowledge that the land where we live, prepare, and share food is located in *Mi'kma'ki*, the ancestral and unceded territory of the Mi'kmaq people. Mi'kma'ki is covered by the Treaties of Peace and Friendship, and as treaty people, we humbly commit to the mutual agreements of peace, respect, and friendship reflected in these living documents.

We recognize the vital role that First Nations, Métis, and Inuit communities play in the stewardship of the lands and waters that sustain our food systems. We also acknowledge the many harms of colonization on Indigenous food systems–including the disruption of traditional knowledge, the dispossession of land, and the erosion of Indigenous foodways and food sovereignty.

At Nourish Nova Scotia, we are committed to honouring and uplifting Indigenous Food Sovereignty through continued learning and relationship-building with Mi'kmaq communities, and by working to support and promote Indigenous-led food systems. As you explore the recipes and content in this book, you will find references to Mi'kmaw language and culture. We invite you to explore this learning further, and reflect on the historical and cultural influences that shape our food systems, what we eat, and our unique connections to food.

CONTENTS

ABOUT THIS COOKBOOK

All proceeds from the sale of this book go directly to supporting school healthy eating programs in Nova Scotia, such as breakfast and snack programs, cooking clubs, and school gardens.

"The kids love coming to the cafeteria every morning and asking every day "what's for lunch?" with the biggest smiles on their faces."

Kim, cafeteria worker

What's For Lunch? is a special family cookbook made by Nourish Nova Scotia with support from the Province of Nova Scotia. It's filled with favourite recipes, fun stories, and colourful artwork, all inspired by school food programs across the province.

At Nourish Nova Scotia, we believe food isn't just about eating—it's about learning, sharing, and discovering new things together. When kids get involved in cooking, they build confidence, make connections, and celebrate where their food comes from. Over the years, we've supported healthy school food through breakfast programs, gardens, cooking activities, and recipe sharing. When the made-from-scratch Nova Scotia School Lunch Program menu launched, we saw an amazing opportunity to keep that energy going–and when we heard that families wanted to cook school meals at home, we thought: Let's turn those delicious favourites into a cookbook!

Cooking together at home is a fun way to try new things, learn cool skills, and enjoy tasty meals as a family. So, we collected the most-loved school recipes—like Handmade Pizza, Chicken Noodle Stir Fry, and Picnic Plates–and added some great breakfast and snack ideas too.

All the recipes in this cookbook follow Nova Scotia's School Food and Nutrition Policy, ensuring they're balanced, wholesome, and kid-approved. Throughout the book, you'll also find special features like *Nutrition Bites* with simple healthy tips, *Local Food Features* that introduce Nova Scotians who grow and produce our food, and *School Food Heroes* who help bring great meals to students across the province.

We hope this cookbook brings joy to your kitchen and inspires you to explore, taste, and share delicious food together.

Nourish Nova Scotia

NOVA SCOTIA

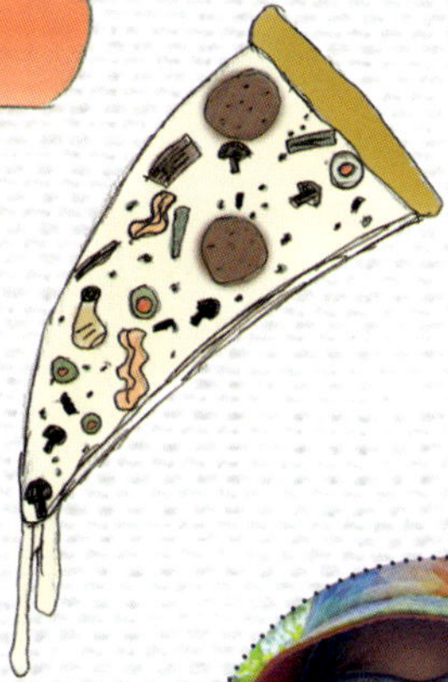

"I have two kids who are in elementary school and are participating in the Nova Scotia School Lunch program. We really like the program because it gives us peace of mind knowing that the kids are having a healthy lunch at school, they come home in a better mood, and they are also more willing to eat things that they didn't want to try before. My ten-year-old, since the program started, is more interested in preparing food and exploring new recipes at home. I think this is a great program that cares about food security, diversity, and equity in the community. I hope the program continues and that kids get to explore recipes and other cultures through food."

Ana, parent

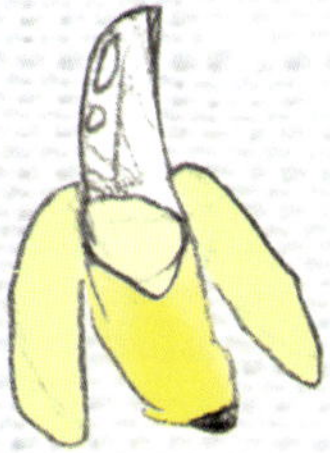

Artwork by Grade 6 students at Oxford School in Halifax.

READY, SET, COOK!

Tips for using this cookbook!

1 **Before you start cooking**, read through the recipe carefully. Make sure you have all the ingredients on hand, understand each step, and have enough time to complete the recipe.

2 If you're wearing long sleeves, **roll them up**, and if you have long hair, **tie it back** to keep it out of your food.

3 **Clear a section of your table** or countertop and clean the area well. Use separate cutting boards for raw meat and other ingredients to prevent cross-contamination.

4 **Wash your hands** with warm soapy water before and after preparing food, and especially after handling raw meat.

5 **Gather all the tools and ingredients** you need to make the recipe.

6 **Get all your ingredients ready.** Chop, peel, or grate anything that needs it, and put them in separate bowls or containers. This is called *mise en place* ("everything in its place"), and is key to making cooking easier and more fun.

7 If you're baking, **have oven mitts ready** and prepare a heat-safe surface to set the hot pan on when it comes out of the oven. This could be a clear stovetop (make sure to move any pots and pans) or a counter with trivets or a cooling rack on top.

8 **Cook, and have fun!** Great cooking skills take time and practice to develop, so don't hesitate to ask for help when you need it. Preparing food together is also a wonderful way to spend time with family and loved ones.

9 **Eat together!**

10 **Clean up.** Store any leftovers promptly. Dispose of all food waste, recycling, and garbage properly. Wash surfaces, kitchen tools, and dishes.

Recipe Ratings

The recipes in this book are rated with *Nourish forks* to show the skill level needed to make them.

- **One fork:** These recipes can be made without using sharp knives or the stove.
- **Two forks:** These recipes involve some chopping and/or cooking on hot surfaces.
- **Three forks:** These recipes are more complex and take longer to make. You might want to ask for help or prepare some parts ahead of time.

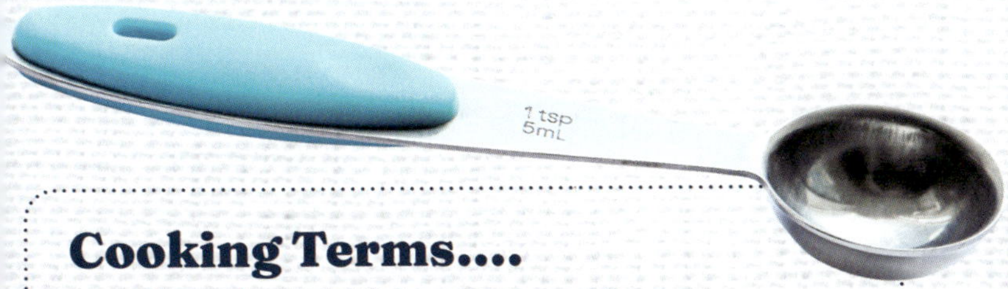

Cooking Terms.... and What They Mean!

BOIL Cook at a full, rolling boil

DICE Chop into ½" pieces (about the width of your fingernail)

FRY Cook food in oil, often until browned

GRATE Carefully rub food against a grater to cut into very small pieces

GREASE Use oil or margarine to make a surface less sticky

MASH Make a cooked vegetable or fruit smooth using a potato masher or fork

MINCE Chop into very small pieces

PEEL Use a vegetable peeler to remove the skin from a fruit or vegetable

PREHEAT Turn the oven on to let it heat up before cooking

SAUTÉ Cook quickly in a little hot fat while stirring

SHRED Cut into long, very thin pieces

SIMMER Cook just below the boiling point

WHISK Use a whisk to beat or stir a mixture

Abbreviations

oz = ounce

lb = pound

tsp = teaspoon

Tbsp = tablespoon

kg = kilogram

ml = millilitre

pkg = package

" = inch *(about 2.5 centimetres)*

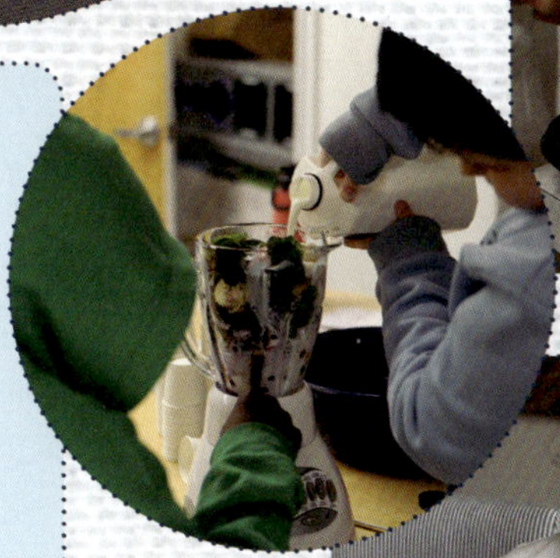

GROWN-UPS, learn more about cooking with kids here:

nourishns.ca/resource/cooking-with-kids/

muffin,
Apple &
Parfait

Morning Glory MUFFINS

MAKES: 12 MUFFINS

Whether you're a seasoned baker or just getting started, these carrot cake–inspired muffins are a great place to practice your skills while letting your imagination run wild. Try using grated parsnip instead of carrots for a surprisingly delicious twist, or add blueberries for a bright explosion of colour! If you'd like some crunch, add ½ cup sunflower or pumpkin seeds to the batter.

What You Need

- 1 cup (250 ml) whole wheat flour
- ½ cup (125 ml) all-purpose flour
- ⅓ cup (80 ml) sugar
- 1 ½ tsp (7.5 ml) baking soda
- 2 tsp (10 ml) cinnamon
- ½ tsp (2.5 ml) salt
- 1 large carrot
- 1 apple
- ⅓ cup (80 ml) shredded coconut
- ⅓ cup (80 ml) raisins, optional
- 2 eggs
- ⅓ cup (80 ml) oil or unsweetened applesauce
- ⅓ cup milk (250 ml)
- ½ tsp (2.5 ml) vanilla

Start Cooking!

1. Preheat the oven to 350°F and grease a muffin pan well or line with muffin liners.
2. In a large bowl, mix the whole wheat flour, all-purpose flour, sugar, baking soda, cinnamon, and salt. Peel the carrot and gently grate it. Grate the apple with its skin on. Place the grated carrot and apple, coconut, and raisins (optional) on top of the flour mixture.
3. In another large bowl, mix eggs, oil or applesauce, milk, and vanilla. Add the wet ingredients to the dry ingredients and mix until just combined.
4. Spoon the batter evenly into the muffin pan. Bake for 15–20 minutes, until a toothpick inserted into the centre of the muffins comes out clean. Carefully remove the muffin pan from the oven with oven mitts and place on a heatproof surface or cooling rack.
5. Cool the muffins before storing in a sealed container or bag at room temperature for up to three days. Freeze for longer storage.

School Kitchen Tips

- If you don't have whole wheat flour, use 1 ½ cups total of all-purpose flour.
- If you don't have a muffin pan, you can bake the muffin mixture in a 9" x 13" pan for 20—25 minutes.
- If the muffin is fully baked, a toothpick inserted into the centre will come out clean.

Make Your Own PARFAITS

MAKES: 4 PARFAITS*

*If using prepared granola.

Students at Oceanview Elementary in Lawrencetown designed this recipe to celebrate the vibrant colours of the Acadian flag. Fruit and Yogurt Parfaits are a School Breakfast Program favourite and are fun to make at home, too. You can use store-bought granola or make your own.

This recipe calls for blueberries, raspberries, and bananas but you can make a delicious parfait using any fresh, canned, or frozen fruit you have on hand.

What You Need

- 1 cup (250 ml) granola, purchased or homemade (see recipe on next page)
- 2 cups (500 ml) yogurt (plain or your favourite flavour)
- 1 banana, sliced
- 1 cup (250 ml) raspberries
- 1 cup (250 ml) blueberries

LET'S MAKE A PARFAIT!

LAYER THE INGREDIENTS IN 4 JARS OR GLASSES IN THIS ORDER:

- 1 heaping spoonful granola
- ¼ cup yogurt
- Banana slices
- 1 heaping spoonful granola
- A small handful raspberries
- ¼ cup yogurt
- A small handful blueberries

Sprinkle any remaining granola, berries, and banana slices on top and serve.

HOMEMADE GRANOLA

Make your own granola and mix it just the way you like by adding your favourite dried fruit and seeds. Quick oats are easiest to chew, but old-fashioned rolled oats work too. Top your granola with milk or yogurt for a quick breakfast, stash a bag in your backpack for an after-school snack, or use it to Make Your Own Parfait!

- 6 cups (1 kg) rolled oats
- ½ tsp (2.5 ml) salt
- 1 cup (250 ml) shredded coconut
- 1 cup (250 ml) sunflower seeds or pumpkin seeds
- ½ cup (125 ml) honey, maple syrup, or sugar
- ½ cup (125 ml) oil
- 1 Tbsp (15 ml) vanilla, optional
- 1 cup (250 ml) or more any dried fruit: dried cranberries, dried blueberries, raisins, sliced dates, sliced dried apricots, or chopped apple chips

Start Cooking!

1. Preheat the oven to 350°F and grease a baking sheet with oil or line with parchment paper. In a large bowl, mix the rolled oats with salt, coconut, and your favourite seeds.
2. In another bowl, whisk the honey, maple syrup, or sugar with the oil and vanilla. Pour the honey mixture over the dry ingredients and stir well to combine.
3. Spread the granola onto a baking sheet and bake at 350°F for 20–30 minutes, stirring every 10 minutes, until the granola is golden brown. Cool, stirring from time to time.
4. Mix in your favourite dried fruit and store in an airtight container at room temperature. Your granola will keep for months stored in a cool place.

"It made the house smell delightful. My favourite way to eat it is on top of yogurt, it's delicious!"
Gabe, Grade 7

Photo credit Jill Eason

Did You Know?

- Granola was invented in 1863 and was the first cold breakfast cereal to be made in a factory. It was originally sold as "Granula" and consisted of hard dry crumbles of graham flour that had to be soaked overnight before eating. We think you'll like this version better!
- Parfait means "perfect" in French.

FARM to School Snack

Tart and sweet dried cranberries are a popular choice in the **Nourish Nova Scotia Farm to School Snack Program**, which brings a burst of local flavour to schools!

Each month, students taste fresh local produce while learning how fruits and vegetables grow. From ground cherries to bell peppers and kale, snacks come with info sheets, fun facts, and videos. Dedicated volunteers run the program with support from our Farm to School Snack Coordinator. To learn more about how the program works, check out: *nourishns.ca/farm-to-school-snack.*

Farm to School Snack
Nourish Nova Scotia

LOCAL FOOD FEATURE: CRANBERRIES

Two generations of the Ernst family at **Terra Beata Farms** grow cranberries in Lunenburg and Kings counties. At their processing plant on Heckmans Island, they produce juice, dried fruit, and cranberry sauce. At their facility in Sackville, New Brunswick, they work with other cranberry farmers to process and ship 5 million pounds of cranberries all over the world each year.

Photo credit: Terra Beata Farms

FUN FACTS!

Cranberries grow on low vines in bogs. Farmers trim the vines and rely on bees for pollination. The vines are perennial and produce berries year after year.

At harvest time the cranberry bogs are flooded and a machine called a beater shakes the ripe berries loose. They float to the surface and are gathered with special tools before being loaded onto trucks.

Cranberries are filled with tiny air pockets and bounce like balls when firm and ripe!

Did You Know?

- Cranberries have been harvested by Indigenous peoples across Turtle Island (North America) for centuries and used for different foods and medicines. When apples were introduced by French settlers, Mi'kmaq named them *wenju'su'n* (wen-jew-soon), which translates to "French cranberry."

PUMPKIN Polka Dot Bars

MAKES: 24 BARS

These colourful and delicious bars adapted from the *Strive for Five!* cookbook are a crowd favourite at Grosvenor-Wentworth Park Elementary School's Breakfast Program.

What You Need

Oil or margarine for greasing the pan

- 1 cup (250 ml) whole wheat flour
- ½ cup (125 ml) all-purpose flour
- ½ cup (125 ml) sugar
- 2 tsp (10 ml) baking powder
- 1 tsp (5 ml) cinnamon
- ½ tsp (2.5 ml) salt
- 1 ½ cups (375 ml) mashed or canned pumpkin (½ of a 798 ml can)
- 2 eggs
- ½ cup (125 ml) oil
- ¼ cup (60 ml) milk
- 1 cup (250 ml) cranberries (fresh, frozen, or dried)

Start Cooking!

1. Let's bake! Preheat the oven to 350°F and lightly grease a baking sheet. In a large bowl, combine the whole wheat flour, all-purpose flour, sugar, baking powder, cinnamon, and salt.
2. In another bowl, whisk together the pumpkin, eggs, oil, and milk.
3. Add the pumpkin mixture to the flour mixture and stir just until combined. Gently stir in the cranberries.
4. Spread the mixture evenly over the prepared pan. It will be quite a thin layer, so try using the back of a wet spoon to spread the mixture. Bake for 25–30 minutes, until a toothpick inserted into the centre comes out clean. Carefully remove from the oven with oven mitts and place on a heatproof surface or cooling rack.
5. Cool and cut into 24 bars. Store bars in a sealed container for up to three days or freeze for longer storage.

School Kitchen Tips

- No whole wheat flour? Use 1 ½ cups all-purpose flour instead.
- Swap pumpkin with mashed squash or sweet potatoes.
- For crunch, sprinkle the batter with sunflower or pumpkin seeds.
- Make it your way with any chopped fruit or berries instead of cranberries!

USE IT UP:
This recipe uses just half a can of pumpkin. Use a spatula to scrape the remainder into a plastic bag and freeze for your next batch of Polka Dot Bars or Mac and Cheese (see recipe on page 50).

SMOOTHIE LAB

MAKES: AS MANY AS YOU LIKE

Many schools across Nova Scotia offer smoothies in their breakfast and snack programs—and for good reason. Smoothies are a nourishing and delicious way to refuel. Making smoothies at home is a fun way to explore new tastes and get creative. Let this guide inspire you to discover your favourite flavour combinations. You may be surprised by what you come up with, so remember to write down your favourite recipes.

Be brave!
Be adventurous!
Be smooth!

How to Make a Smoothie

Simply use a blender to combine 2–3 options from each of these ingredient categories below. Blend for at least 1 minute, until very smooth. Taste it, and if you think it needs a little more of something, add it and blend again.

If experimenting with friends or family, have each person build and blend their unique smoothie one at a time, rinsing the blender between turns. Pour everyone a taste of each smoothie. Which mix of flavours did you like best?

FRESH OR FROZEN FRUIT

Use about ½ cup (125 ml) per smoothie

Berries, cherries, peaches, pineapple, mango, banana, oranges, kiwi, apple, lemon

VEGETABLES

Use about ½ cup (125 ml) per smoothie

Fresh baby spinach (frozen does not work well), avocado, carrots, kale, beets, cooked pumpkin, cooked sweet potato

HERBS AND SPICES

Start with about ¼ tsp (1.25 ml) per smoothie

Fresh or dried ginger, cinnamon, turmeric, cocoa powder, cacao nibs, fresh parsley, basil

NUTS AND SEEDS

Use about 1 Tbsp (15 ml) per smoothie

Hemp hearts, chia seeds, ground flax seeds, sunflower seeds, almond butter, sunflower butter, peanut butter

PROTEIN

Use about ½ cup (125 ml) per smoothie

Greek yogurt or regular yogurt, cottage cheese, cooked white beans, silken tofu

SWEETENERS

Use 1 tsp to 1 Tbsp (5–15 ml) per smoothie

Maple syrup, honey, pitted dates

LIQUIDS

Start with about ½ cup (125 ml) per smoothie and add more if needed

Fruit juice, coconut water, coconut milk, oat milk, almond milk, soy milk, cow's milk, goat's milk, iced tea

Write Your Favourite Smoothie Recipe Here:

"The kids were engaged and having fun! It was clear that some of the kids felt some real ownership when in the kitchen and that was great to see. I think that we have some budding chefs on our hands."

SchoolsPlus staff

"Delightful and delicious!"

Claire, Grade 1

The Smoothie Lab is one of Nourish Nova Scotia's Youth Food Skills workshops, designed to teach youth essential skills like cooking, growing food, and practicing food safety.

Youth Food Leaders

Nourish Nova Scotia

Creamy POTATO SOUP

MAKES: 6–8 BOWLS

This rich and comforting potato soup is a perfect balance of creamy texture and deep, savoury flavour. The combination of tender potatoes, sweet onions, and sharp cheddar cheese creates a velvety base, while fresh chives add a delicious contrast in texture and taste. This soup pairs beautifully with a slice of crusty bread or a simple side salad for a well-rounded meal. No wonder it's a favourite with the students at the Karma Closet Free Lunch program at Northumberland Regional High! For a dairy-free soup, simply leave out the cheese and use oil to cook the onions.

What You Need

- 1 large onion
- 3 lb (1.36 kg) baking potatoes (about 6)
- 2 Tbsp (30 ml) margarine or oil
- 4 ½ cups (1.13 L) water
- 1 tsp (5 ml) salt
- ½ lb (225 g) cheddar cheese, grated (about 1 ½ cups, 375 ml)
- ¼ cup (60 ml) chopped chives or green onions, for serving

Start Cooking!

1. Peel and mince the onion. Peel, rinse, and chop the potatoes into 1″ pieces.
2. In a large pot, heat the margarine or oil on medium-low. Add the onion and cook, stirring occasionally, until translucent, about five minutes. Stir in the potatoes, water, and salt and bring to a boil.
3. Reduce the heat, cover, and simmer, stirring occasionally, until the potatoes are very tender, 15–20 minutes. Remove the pot from the heat and carefully mash some of the potatoes.
4. Return the pan to the heat and add the cheese, stirring until melted. Remove the pan from the heat. Taste the soup and add more salt if needed. Serve the soup topped with the chives or green onions. Refrigerate leftovers promptly. Any leftover Potato Soup can be stored in the refrigerator for up to three days.

FUN FACTS!

Potatoes have been grown in space!

There are over 4,000 different varieties of potatoes worldwide in various shades of pink, yellow, orange, purple, and blue.

Did You Know?

- Some people say that the famous Nova Scotian nickname “Bluenose” originally came from the blue-streaked potatoes that were once a staple crop in the Annapolis Valley!

School Food Heroes

This recipe comes straight from the Karma Closet Free Lunch Program kitchen at Northumberland Regional High School in Alma. Every day, sixteen young cooks in the Culinary 11 class prepare a meal for up to two hundred of their fellow students.

Working with their teachers, Karen Berezowski and Paul Heighton, these chefs-in-training offer soups, a salad bar, and hearty dishes like Potato Soup, Macaroni and Cheese, Lemon Chicken, Black Bean Tacos, and Greek Pasta Salad.

Awarded with Chignecto Central Regional Centre for Education’s Exemplary Values Award in 2025, this free lunch program has been an inspiration not only in this province, but for all of Canada. When the National School Food Policy was announced in June 2024, Northumberland High welcomed the Prime Minister and Minister of Families, Children & Social Development to make the announcement.

The school’s agriculture classes even grow fresh potatoes, tomatoes, microgreens, and lettuce to use in the meals. We’re so happy they shared their recipe for their famous Potato Soup.

The Nova Scotia SCHOOL LUNCH PROGRAM

Every student deserves a healthy meal—not just to nourish their body, but to support their learning, growth, and sense of belonging. This commitment to students is at the heart of Nova Scotia's School Lunch Program, which began rolling out in schools across the province in October 2024.

This program was created to ensure every student has access to a nutritious meal every school day. It's about more than just food and hunger. It's about helping kids feel ready to learn, able to focus, and fully included in a way that's welcoming and free of stigma.

There's no one-size-fits-all solution, so the program is built with flexibility. Some schools prepare meals in their own kitchens. Others work with local food service vendors, who either cook on-site or deliver meals each day. No matter the approach, the goal remains the same: a nourishing meal for every child.

Families can confidentially choose what to pay. Participation is encouraged for everyone.

This work is only possible thanks to a dedicated team of school staff, food service providers, community volunteers, government partners, and behind-the-scenes School Food Leads—all of whom bring care, creativity, and heart to school food, every single day.

The impact is already clear. By January 2025, more than 2 million lunches had been served across 258 schools. That's 2 million moments of support, connection, and nourishment. When students are well-fed, they're ready to learn, and that benefits us all.

From the Department of Education and Early Childhood Development

"Built with love by Nova Scotia, our school lunch program is making life more affordable for families and fuelling kids to learn with bellies full of delicious, nutritious food. I'm so proud of the work so many have done to make this a reality for students and families."

Becky Druhan, Minister of Education and Early Childhood Development 2021–2024

"As a parent today, I can provide lunch for my kids—but I grew up in a food-insecure home, and I know first-hand what it's like to go to school hungry. When I read the school's message that all students would be fed, regardless of their ability to pay, I felt an unexpected wave of relief—not for me, but for the kids and families who need it most. This program will be incredibly impactful. It is more than just food; it's security, dignity, and a better chance to learn and thrive."

Jemima, parent

Salad Bar

Maple Blueberry FRENCH TOAST BAKE

MAKES: 6 PIECES

This Maple Blueberry French Toast Bake is a variation of French Toast. Instead of dipping individual slices of bread into an egg mixture and frying them, we bake up a pan full of bread cubes with a maple custard mixture and blueberries. If you don't have blueberries, substitute one or two diced apples.

French Toast Bake is delicious with berries or the Sautéed Apples (recipe on page 24).

Note: For best results, start this recipe the day before you plan to serve it.

What You Need

- Margarine or cooking spray for greasing the pan
- 6 eggs
- ¾ cup (175 ml) milk
- 1 tsp (5 ml) vanilla extract
- 2 Tbsp (30 ml) maple syrup or brown sugar
- ½ tsp (2.5 ml) cinnamon
- ¼ tsp (1.25 ml) nutmeg
- ⅛ tsp (.65 ml) salt
- ½ lb (227 g) whole wheat bread (about half a loaf)
- 1 ½ cups (375 ml) fresh or frozen blueberries

FOR THE TOPPING

- 2 Tbsp (30 ml) maple syrup or brown sugar

FUN FACTS!

Pkwimann (pgwee-mun), wild blueberries, are native to Turtle Island (North America) and have been growing naturally in Nova Scotia for more than ten thousand years.

Cultivated, or "highbush" blueberries, which are larger and sweeter, have been grown on commercial farms for just over one hundred years.

USE IT UP

Dice and freeze stale bread, bagels, English muffins, leftover biscuits, or Lu'skinikn until you have about 5 cups to make this recipe.

Start Baking!

1. Grease a 9 x 13" baking pan with margarine or spray well with cooking spray. In a large bowl, whisk together the eggs, milk, vanilla, 2 Tbsp maple syrup or brown sugar, cinnamon, nutmeg, and salt.
2. Cut or tear the bread into ½" pieces. Add the blueberries and bread to the egg mixture and stir to combine.
3. Pour the mixture into the baking pan. Cover with foil and let stand at room temperature for one hour, or refrigerate overnight.
4. Preheat the oven to 350°F. If you are using brown sugar instead of maple syrup for the topping, sprinkle it over the French Toast Bake and put the foil cover back on. Bake for 25 minutes. Carefully remove the foil with oven mitts and bake for 10–15 more minutes, until golden brown.
5. Carefully remove from the oven with oven mitts and place on a heatproof surface. If topping with maple syrup, drizzle it over the bake while it is still warm. Cut into six pieces and serve. Leftover French Toast Bake can be refrigerated for up to three days.

"Personally, I love the lunches that are in the program, especially the French Toast!"
Grade 4 student

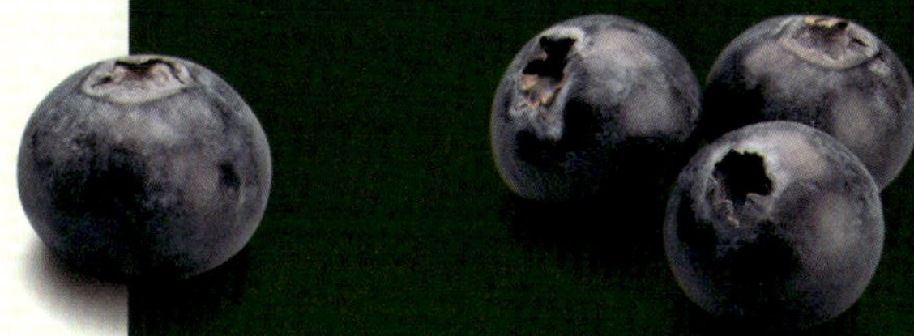

Did You Know?

- Mi'kmaq have been harvesting the sap of *snawey* (snah-way), the sugar maple, and making maple sugar for thousands of years. Maple sugar has a much longer shelf life than maple syrup due to its lower water content, so in the days before refrigeration, the syrup was a special treat to enjoy during the boiling process.
- In the Mi'kmaw calendar, the March moon is known as *Siwkewiku's* (Siwk-a-we-goose), the Spring Time Moon, also known as the Maple Sugar Moon.
- In summer, maple trees make their own food and store it as sap in their roots for winter. When spring comes, the sap moves up the tree. People drill small holes to collect the sap, then boil it to make yummy maple syrup!

Indigenous Foods Coordinator Sakej Doucette teaching youth how to harvest maple sap

LOCAL FOOD FEATURE: BLUEBERRIES

During blueberry harvest around July, you can find blueberries at a farm stand or U-pick like **Oxford Berry Farm** in Cumberland County. When they're not in season, look for frozen Nova Scotian wild blueberries at a grocery store near you. Famous for their sweet taste and vibrant colour, they're a local favourite in jams, pies, and blueberry grunt. Nova Scotia produces about 40–60 million pounds of blueberries each year!

Big Batch BREAKFAST SANDWICHES

MAKES: 12 SANDWICHES

This recipe, adapted from the South Shore Regional Centre for Education, is a simple way to make a big batch of delicious breakfast sandwiches. Refrigerate any leftovers and you'll have a quick breakfast to grab on the way to school. Experiment with flavours by switching up the vegetables or adding your favourite cooked lean meat.

"Since the start of the lunch program, we have become a bigger team in the kitchen. I just love the feeling that we're all working together to make meals for so many of our students!"

Cafeteria worker

What You Need

You will need 2 baking sheets with sides (cookie sheets)

- Margarine or oil to grease the pan
- 12 eggs
- ½ tsp (2.5 ml) salt
- ½ cup (125 ml) milk
- 1 small onion or 2 tsp (10 ml) onion powder
- 1 red or green bell pepper
- 1 large handful fresh or ½ cup cooked spinach
- 1 cup (100 g) grated cheddar or mozzarella cheese
- 12 English muffins, whole wheat if you like
- 2 Tbsp (30 ml) margarine for spreading

Try pairing this recipe for warm, spiced apples with the Breakfast Sandwich or French Toast Bake.

SAUTÉED APPLES

- 2 large or 3 medium apples
- 1 Tbsp (15 ml) margarine
- ½ tsp (2.5 ml) cinnamon
- ¼ tsp (1.25 ml) ground ginger
- 2 Tbsp (30 ml) water

Wash, core, and dice the apples. Heat a frying pan to medium-high and add the margarine. Once it has melted, add the apples. Stir and cook for 2–3 minutes, then add the cinnamon, ginger, and water. Continue to stir and cook for 4–5 minutes longer, or until the water has evaporated and the apples are slightly softened. Serve right away or refrigerate for up to three days.

Start Cooking!

1. Let's get cracking! Preheat the oven to 400°F. Spray one of the baking sheets with cooking spray or grease with margarine or oil.

2. Carefully crack the eggs into a large bowl. Add the salt, milk, and onion powder (if using fresh onion, see step 3 instead) and beat until smooth with a whisk or a fork.

3. Mince the onion (if using onion powder, see step 2 instead), dice the bell pepper, and chop the spinach. Pour the egg mixture onto the prepared baking sheet. Sprinkle the minced onion, peppers, spinach, and cheese evenly over the eggs.

4. Being careful not to spill, place the baking sheet into the oven and set the timer for 12 minutes.

5. While the eggs are cooking, split the English muffins in half and spread each half with a little margarine. Place them on the second baking sheet cut side up. After 12 minutes, check the eggs. They should be "set" in the middle, or fully cooked (no longer liquid or raw). If not, put them back in the oven for a few more minutes.

6. When the eggs are cooked, use oven mitts to remove them from the oven and set aside on a heatproof surface. Place the baking sheet of English muffins in the oven for 6–7 minutes, until heated and beginning to toast. Carefully remove the pan of English muffins from the oven.

7. Cut the egg sheet into 12 equal pieces. Place each piece on half an English muffin, then top with another half and serve. Refrigerate leftovers promptly in a sealed container or freeze for longer storage. To reheat, microwave refrigerated sandwiches for about 1 minute and frozen sandwiches for about 2 minutes.

School Kitchen Tips

- To make six breakfast sandwiches, divide all ingredients in half and bake the egg mixture in an 8" x 8" baking pan. The cooking time will be a bit less, about 10 minutes.
- Substitute toasted bread or bagels for the English muffins to change things up. You can also roll your egg patty into a tortilla to make a Breakfast Wrap.
- Our recipe tester Liam, Grade 12, suggests spreading each English muffin with a bit of strawberry jam and using a cookie cutter to cut the egg mixture into a circle.

FUN FACTS!

Apple trees were first planted in the Annapolis Valley by French settlers in the 1600s.

Apples are part of the rose family, and apple trees have beautiful rose-like blossoms.

RAPPIE PIE

MAKES: 12 PIECES

In Conseil scolaire acadien provincial and Tri-County Regional Centre for Education schools, *pâté à la râpure*, or Rappie Pie, is served regularly. This golden-brown treat is a traditional Acadian dish in many areas of the Maritimes.

Rappie pie is best known for its distinctive texture and delicious flavour, and is made with simple ingredients and a lot of care. Some like their râpure on the runny side while others prefer a more dense consistency. If you like your rappie pie more soupy than solid, use the larger amount of water when making the broth.

What You Need

- 2 onions
- 1 whole chicken (about 3–4 lb)
- 1 Tbsp (15 ml) salt
- ¼ tsp (1.25 ml) black pepper
- 14–16 cups (3.5–4 L) water
- 2 Tbsp (30 ml) salted green onions, optional
- 2 lb (900 g) frozen rappie pie mix, defrosted
- 1 cup (250 ml) cold water
- 2 Tbsp (30 ml) margarine or butter

YOUR CHOICE OF TOPPINGS
margarine or butter, molasses, pickles, chow chow, cranberry sauce, applesauce

Did You Know?

Chicken is a popular rappie pie filling, but it can also be made with beef, seafood, or rabbit!

Caution

You will need a very large metal or ceramic baking pan or two smaller pans. This is a big project with hot liquid, so you will want to work with a grown-up!

Start Cooking!

1 Peel and dice the onions. Place the onions and the chicken in a stockpot and add the salt, black pepper, and water. Bring to a boil over high heat, then reduce the heat to simmer and cook until the chicken is tender and pulls easily from the bones, about 1-2 hours.

2 Remove the pot from the heat and let it stand until it is cool enough to remove the chicken without danger of burning yourself. Remove the chicken to a platter and set the stock aside. Pick the chicken meat from the bones, chop into ½″ pieces, and refrigerate. Note: To save time, this step can be done a day ahead. In this case, let stock cool to room temperature and refrigerate it until you are ready to cook.

3 When you are ready to proceed, bring the stock to a boil. Grease a large casserole dish or rappie pie pan with the margarine or spray with cooking spray (if you don't have a large pan, use two 9″ x 13″ pans). Preheat the oven to 400°F.

4 In a very large bowl place the defrosted rappie pie mix. Add 1 cup of cold water and blend with a potato masher until smooth. Sprinkle in the salted green onions if using. Carefully add the hot stock 1 or 2 cups at a time, stirring after each addition until well incorporated. When almost all the stock has been added, taste the mixture, and add a little more salt, pepper, or salted green onions if needed. Add the remaining stock and stir for a few minutes.

5 Pour half of the potato mixture into the pan. Spread the chicken pieces over the potato layer, then evenly pour the remaining potato mixture over the chicken.

6 Bake for 2–3 hours, until the crust is nicely browned. Let rest for at least 10 minutes before serving with butter and molasses.

School Kitchen Tips

- Every rappie pie cook has their own preferred baking method. Some start with a 400°F oven for one hour, then reduce the temperature to 300°F until the rappie pie is done.
- If you'd like to simplify the preparation, substitute 12 cups chicken stock and 2 lb cooked diced chicken for the whole chicken, salt, and water. Bring the stock to a boil with the diced onions and black pepper, then proceed with step 3. Dot the top of the Rappie Pie with 2 Tbsp margarine or butter before baking.
- Leftover Rappie Pie is excellent heated in an air fryer or in a frying pan!

School Food Heroes

Special thanks to Arlene Drew, Paul Thimot, Kris Gaudet, Sophie Mathieu-Gauthier, Meteghan Râpure, and the team at École Notre Dame de l'Annonciation for sharing their tips to Rappie Pie-making success!

Potato grater and press for making râpure at La Vieille Maison in Meteghan

Did You Know?

Salting green onions and other herbs is a way of preserving fresh herb flavour throughout the winter, and is practiced in many parts of French-speaking Canada. Salted green onions are sold in jars in many regions of Nova Scotia and are fun to make yourself. Find instructions online, or in Simon Thibault's cookbook, *Pantry and Palate: Remembering and Rediscovering Acadian Food.*

Sweet & Sour MEATBALLS

MAKES: 4-6 PLATES

This dish, which is inspired by Chinese Canadian cuisine, has been on the menu in many Nova Scotian homes for decades. At school, the sauce is often made with crushed pineapple to make sure everyone gets their fair share, but at home you can use pineapple tidbits or freshly cut pineapple, diced apples, or peaches with an extra ¼ cup water. This dish is best served with cooked rice or potatoes.

What You Need

FOR THE MEATBALLS

- 1 small onion or 2 tsp (10 ml) onion powder
- 1 clove garlic or 1 tsp (5 ml) garlic powder
- 1 lb (454 g) lean ground beef
- 1 cup (250 ml) cooked lentils, drained and mashed (about half a 540 ml can)
- ⅓ cup (80 ml) ground oatmeal or bread crumbs
- 1 egg
- 1 tsp (7.5 ml) salt
- ¼ tsp (1.25 ml) pepper
- 1 Tbsp (15 ml) oil

FOR THE VEGETABLES

- 1 large or 2 medium carrots
- 1 red or green pepper
- ½ bunch broccoli
- 1 Tbsp (15 ml) oil
- Pinch salt

FOR THE SAUCE

- 1 (398 ml) can crushed pineapple or pineapple tidbits with juice
- ½ cup (125 ml) ketchup
- 3 Tbsp (45 ml) white or apple cider vinegar
- ⅓ cup (80 ml) honey or sugar
- 1 Tbsp (15ml) soy sauce, lower sodium if possible
- ¼ tsp (1.25 ml) powdered ginger or 1 tsp grated fresh ginger, optional
- ¼ cup (60 ml) water
- 1 Tbsp (15 ml) cornstarch

TO SERVE: Cooked rice or mashed potatoes

Start Cooking!

1. To make the meatballs, preheat the oven to 400°F. Peel the onion if using fresh and mince or grate it. Mince the garlic if using fresh. In a large bowl, combine the ground meat with the lentils, onion or onion powder, garlic or garlic powder, oatmeal or bread crumbs, egg, salt, and pepper. Use a spoon or clean hands to mix until very well combined, then mix a little more.

2. Spread a baking sheet with 1 Tbsp oil. Roll the meat mixture into balls about ¾" in diameter and place them on the oiled baking sheet.

3. Cook the vegetables: peel the carrot and slice it thinly. Seed and chop or slice the red or green pepper. Cut the broccoli into small florets. On a second baking sheet, toss the vegetables with 1 Tbsp oil and a pinch of salt.

4. Bake the meatballs and veggies for about 15–20 minutes, or until the meatballs are cooked through (a thermometer inserted into a meatball should read at least 165°F) and the veggies are tender, but still crisp.

5. Make the sauce: while the meatballs and veggies are cooking, combine the pineapple with all its liquid, ketchup, vinegar, honey or sugar, soy sauce, and ginger in a small pot. Bring to a simmer over medium-high heat. Whisk the water with the cornstarch and add to the pineapple mixture. Cook and stir until the mixture bubbles and thickens.

6. When the meatballs and vegetables are cooked, carefully take them out of the oven with oven mitts and place on a heatproof surface. Serve the meatballs and veggies with rice or potatoes and spoon on as much sauce as you like.

7. Refrigerate leftovers promptly. Meatballs may be refrigerated for up to three days or frozen for longer storage.

School Kitchen Tips

- Ground pork or chicken can be used in place of the ground beef, or serve the sauce and veggies with fried cubes of boneless pork, chicken, or tofu.
- If you're short on time, simply crumble the meat mixture onto the baking sheet and cook as directed.
- If you don't want to use lentils, simply use 1 ½ lb (680g) lean ground meat.
- The sheet pan method makes this recipe a bit easier, but feel free to stir-fry the vegetables.

"The best things about the lunch program are: It's pay what you can, we get to pick our toppings, you grab and go, and you don't have to wait in a long line!"

Grade 4 student

School Food Story

Chinese Canadian culinary traditions began taking shape around the 1850s, developed by Chinese cooks who had primarily immigrated from Guangdong, a southern province of China. They adapted the flavours of traditional Chinese dishes to suit local tastes and to work with the limited ingredients available at the time. Recipes like Chop Suey, Ginger Beef, General Tso's Chicken, and Sweet and Sour Pork were shared among Chinese restaurant owners across the country, giving rise to a uniquely Canadian and much-loved cuisine. You can learn more about this history in *Chop Suey Nation* by Anhua Xu!

Did You Know?

Combining ground meat with other ingredients, like eggs and mashed lentils, is called a "meat emulsion." This is the same process that gives sausages and donair meat their distinctive texture. Mixing very well produces meatballs that are firm, even with all the additional ingredients you're adding.

CHICKEN NUGGETS & Potato Wedges

MAKES: 4 PLATES

If you love crispy breaded chicken and fries, try this homemade version! Don't worry if you are missing one or two of the herbs and spices for the crumb mixture and potato wedges, they will still turn out great.

If your oven is too small for both baking sheets to fit easily, you can fry the nuggets in a lightly oiled pan over medium heat until cooked through.

What You Need

FOR THE POTATO WEDGES

- 1 lb (454 g) potatoes (about 4 medium potatoes)
- 4 tsp (20 ml) oil
- ¼ tsp (1.25 ml) salt
- ¼ tsp (1.25 ml) black pepper
- ¼ tsp (1.25 ml) garlic powder
- ¼ tsp (1.25 ml) onion powder
- ½ tsp (2.5 ml) dried parsley

FOR THE CHICKEN

- Oil or cooking spray for the pan
- 1 cup (250 ml) fine bread crumbs
- ¼ tsp (1.25 ml) paprika
- ⅛ tsp (0.65 ml) black pepper
- ¼ tsp (1.25 ml) garlic powder
- ¼ tsp (1.25 ml) onion powder
- ¼ tsp (1.25 ml) dried parsley
- 2 Tbsp (30 ml) oil, divided
- 1 lb (454 g) boneless, skinless chicken breast
- ½ tsp (2.5 ml) salt

TO SERVE: cooked peas tossed with margarine, carrot sticks, cucumber slices or pepper slices, ketchup

USE IT UP
Leftover chicken nuggets are great in wraps.

Start Cooking!

1 **To make the potato wedges**, preheat the oven to 400°F and line a baking sheet with parchment paper. Cut the potatoes into thin wedges (8–10 wedges per potato) and place them in a large bowl.

2 Drizzle the wedges with 4 tsp oil, then sprinkle with the salt, black pepper, garlic powder, onion powder, and dried parsley. Toss with a spoon or clean hands until the potatoes are evenly coated with the spices and oil.

3 Spread the wedges out on the baking sheet, in a single layer, then bake on the middle oven rack for 45–50 minutes, until golden and tender.

4 **Meanwhile, make the chicken**. Grease a second baking sheet with oil or cooking spray. Combine the bread crumbs, paprika, black pepper, garlic powder, onion powder, dried parsley, and 1 Tbsp oil in a bowl. Whisk well to combine.

5 Carefully cut the chicken breasts into bite-sized pieces, about the size of your thumb, and place them in a large bowl. Add remaining 1 Tbsp oil and the salt, then stir to coat the pieces of chicken evenly. One at a time, coat the chicken pieces in the crumbs and place them on the baking sheet in a single layer. Remember to wash your hands well after breading the chicken.

6 Place the pan of nuggets on the lower oven rack, and bake for 15 minutes. Carefully flip the chicken pieces with tongs or a fork and return to the oven. Bake for 5–10 minutes longer, until the chicken is cooked through and no longer pink inside when you carefully cut into a piece.

7 Serve the chicken nuggets and potato wedges with cooked peas or raw veggies and ketchup. Leftover chicken nuggets and potato wedges can be refrigerated for up to three days.

School Kitchen Tips

- Use one clean hand for picking up the raw chicken, and the other hand to bread the chicken. That way your fingers won't get coated in the process.
- 1 lb chicken is about 2 medium chicken breasts
- Chicken nuggets may be made ahead and refrigerated for up to 3 days or frozen for up to 3 months. When baking from frozen, increase the baking time by 5–10 minutes, until the chicken is cooked through and no longer pink inside when you carefully cut into a piece.

Nutrition Bites

Fat is an important part of the foods we eat: it gives us energy, helps us to use important vitamins, and supports our growing brains. It also adds flavour and the perfect texture to our recipes. Canola oil, olive oil, and soft margarine can be great everyday choices. And when you're enjoying something comforting like a slice of bread fresh from the oven, adding butter can make it extra special.

Did You Know?

The Mi'kmaw word for potato is *tapatat* (dub-a-dut). Try saying it!

Sipekne'katik is the name of both a traditional region and one of 13 Mi'kmaw communities in Nova Scotia and means "where wild potatoes are found".

Beef & Bean TACOS

MAKES: 12 TACOS

Tacos originated in Mexico, where toppings include *carnitas* (shredded pork), *frijoles* (beans), and *barbacoa* (slow-cooked lamb or beef). These soft-shell tacos have a beef and bean filling and are as quick to make as a taco kit. At school, tacos are often served with corn and rice. Some schools even offer a salad bar where students can top their tacos to their liking, just like at home!

What You Need

- 1 onion, diced, or 2 tsp (10 ml) onion powder
- 1 clove garlic, minced or 1 tsp (5 ml) garlic powder
- 1 Tbsp (15 ml) oil
- 1 lb (454 g) lean ground beef
- 2 Tbsp (30 ml) chili powder
- ½ teaspoon (2.5 ml) salt
- 1 (540 ml) can lentils, kidney beans, or black beans or 2 cups (500 ml) cooked beans, mashed with a bit of cooking liquid
- ½ cup (125 ml) prepared salsa, optional
- 12 small whole wheat or corn tortillas

SIDES AND TOPPINGS OF YOUR CHOICE
cooked rice, corn, chopped raw or cooked peppers, shredded cabbage or lettuce, diced tomatoes, minced onion, salsa, sour cream, grated cheese, chopped pineapple, minced cilantro, hot sauce

FUN FACT!

Did you know that corn tortillas are made with masa, a dough made from ground corn softened with an alkaline solution, such as slaked lime or wood ash? Learn more on page 41.

Start Cooking!

1. If using fresh, peel and dice the onion and mince the garlic. If using onion powder and garlic powder, skip to the next step.

2. Heat the oil in a large pan over medium heat and add the ground beef, onions (or onion powder), garlic (or garlic powder), chili powder, and salt. Cook and stir until beef has browned, about 10–15 minutes.

3. Add the lentils or mashed beans and optional salsa. Cook, stirring occasionally, until the mixture bubbles. Reduce heat to low and cook for another 10 minutes or so, until most of the liquid has evaporated and the mixture has thickened. Meanwhile, prepare any toppings you'd like to serve and arrange on a tray or place in individual bowls.

4. Warm the tortillas in the microwave or toaster oven. Fill the tortillas with the beef mixture and serve with the toppings so everyone can make their tacos to their taste.

5. Promptly refrigerate leftovers. Leftover beef mixture can be stored tightly covered in the refrigerator for up to three days or frozen for longer storage.

"I teach Grade 5, and the lunch program is going great! Students love trying new foods and get excited for favourites like soft-shell tacos. The salad bar is a big hit, and every student gets lunch—no scrambling, no questions asked"

Julian, Grade 5 teacher

School Kitchen Tips

- Dried beans are budget-friendly but need extra prep. Soak overnight, then boil and simmer 1–2 hours until tender. Blow on a bean–if the skin peels, it's ready!
- If you have ground cumin, try sprinkling in a bit while the beef is cooking. Chili powder already contains cumin but a little extra will give your tacos more punch.
- Make vegetarian tacos by using 2 cans (4 cups) of beans and omitting the beef.

LOCAL FOOD FEATURE: BEANS

Wikunn (we-goon), beans, are native to Turtle Island (North America), with a great diversity of varieties cultivated by Indigenous peoples. **Webster Farms** in Cambridge grows about 180,000 pounds of dried beans yearly on 170 acres of farmland. Annapolis Valley First Nation owns the nearly 300-year-old farm, which also produces rhubarb, raspberries, and strawberries. Webster Farms produces three varieties of beans: Yellow-Eye, Jacob's Cattle, and Soldier.

Photo credit: Webster Farms

Nutrition Bites

Meat like chicken breast, lean ground beef, and turkey can help your body stay strong and full of energy! These foods are packed with protein to keep your muscles strong, plus important nutrients like iron and B vitamins that help you feel your best. Lean meats are easy to use in all kinds of meals, and are a tasty way to add extra nutrition to your plate. Foods like black beans or tofu are awesome plant-based choices that can be just as tasty and nourishing.

Grow a WINDOWSILL GARDEN

Have you ever tried growing your own food? Even if you don't have a yard, you can easily grow a garden on your windowsill!

Microgreens are the seedlings of edible vegetables and herbs. They taste like a miniature version of the plant they grow into. Growing microgreens is easy and fun. They can be grown all year round in a window or under a grow light. The microgreens can take anywhere from a few days to three weeks to grow, depending on the plant types you select.

Grow Eat Learn
Nourish Nova Scotia

Nourish Nova Scotia's Grow Eat Learn Program provides support, mentorship, and resources for building gardens and growing spaces on school grounds in Nova Scotia. Learn more at: *nourishns.ca/grow-eat-learn*

What You Need

- Shallow container with drainage holes (you can use a plastic salad or fruit package, or punch holes in a paper milk carton laid on its side)
- Larger container or tray (to prevent mess)
- Potting soil
- Seeds such as arugula, basil, parsley, broccoli, buckwheat, cabbage, or peas
- Plastic wrap
- Light and heat (window sill or grow light)
- Spray bottle
- Scissors

Start Growing!

1. Fill the container with about 2 inches (5 cm) of moistened potting mix soil and press it down gently to create an even surface.
2. Sprinkle seeds evenly over the soil and gently press them in. Cover the seeds with a fine layer of dry potting soil.
3. Put the container on a large tray to prevent a mess. Gently spray water over the newly planted seeds. Cover the container with plastic wrap or a clear plastic lid and place it in a warm, sunny location. The greens will need at least 4 hours of direct sunlight per day to thrive.
4. Use a mister to keep the soil moist. Spray 1–2 times per day until sprouts appear (3–7 days). When the sprouts emerge, remove the plastic cover and continue to moisten them 1–2 times per day. Microgreens are most nutrient rich when the first leaf (the cotyledon, or seed leaf) has fully developed. Harvest your greens by cutting them with scissors at the base of the stem. Wash and gently dry the greens before adding to your wraps, sandwiches, salads, and hot meals.

Year-Round School Gardens

Caledonia Junior High and Admiral Westphal Elementary Schools in Dartmouth make great use of hydroponic and vertical gardens in their classrooms. In these small indoor spaces, students are able to grow lettuce, herbs, tomatoes, microgreens, and cucumbers. Students also sell seedlings to the community as a fundraiser, using their indoor garden as a baby plant nursery.

The gardening clubs at both schools have big plans for the future! They will be planting pollinator gardens and building raised beds outdoors, and one day they hope to purchase a geodesic dome greenhouse to grow even more food year-round.

Photo credit: Hilary Briar

Build-Your-Own CHICKEN RANCH WRAP

MAKES: 6 WRAPS

This is a choose-your-own-adventure version of the Chicken Ranch Wrap served at school, shared by Chignecto Central Regional Centre for Education. Everyone in the family can choose what to put on their wrap. To make a vegetarian wrap, spread the tortilla with some hummus (see recipe on page 39) before adding the dressing and veggies.

What You Need

- 1 lb (454 g) boneless skinless chicken breast
- ½ tsp (2.5 ml) salt
- 1 large carrot
- 1 small head Romaine or leaf lettuce
- 1 cup (250 ml) shredded cheddar cheese
- 6 large whole wheat tortillas
- ¾ cup (185 ml) **Ranch Dressing** (see recipe for Ranch Dip on page 39)

SIDES AND TOPPINGS OF YOUR CHOICE
Sliced peppers, cucumber, tomato, red onion, pickles

FUN FACTS!

Carrots come in a variety of shapes, sizes, and colours, including orange, red, purple, yellow, and white.

The Mi'kmaw word for carrot is *wisawipuneksit* (wee-sow-we-boon-ek-sit).

Start Cooking!

1. Place the chicken in a baking dish and season with the salt. If you have time, refrigerate the chicken overnight.

2. Preheat the oven to 350°F and bake the chicken for 20–30 minutes, until it is no longer pink inside when you carefully cut into it. A thermometer inserted into the thickest part of the breast should read at least 165°F. When the chicken is cool, dice it and refrigerate until needed.

3. Peel and grate the carrot. Wash and thinly shred the lettuce. Prepare the additional toppings of your choice. Place the prepared vegetables and cheese plus your choice of toppings in bowls or on a cookie sheet.

4. Lay out the tortillas, dressing, cooked chicken, and toppings on a counter, leaving plenty of room to build your wrap.

5. Starting with a tortilla laid out flat in front of you, add 2–3 Tbsp dressing in a line near the middle. Layer chicken, cheese, lettuce, carrots, and your choice of toppings, allowing space on all sides for folding. Fold in one or two sides of the tortilla, then starting from the bottom, roll it up as firmly as you can.

6. Serve the wraps right away or refrigerate for up to three days. Wraps are best served within a day or two of rolling.

Nutrition Bites

Veggies help your body stay strong and healthy. They're loaded with things your body loves, like energy, fibre, and nutrients that keep you feeling great. Try adding a few veggies to your meals and see which ones you like best. You don't have to eat a bunch all at once! Every time you try something new is a great step to filling half your plate with colourful plants.

LOCAL FOOD FEATURE: CARROTS

In Nova Scotia, farmers plant carrot seeds in spring, and after 2–3 months, they're ready to pick! The crunchy part grows underground, while leafy greens grow on top. **Elmridge Farm** in Centreville grows sweet carrots and other veggies, and are featured in Nourish Nova Scotia's Farm to Snack Adventures video series. Check it out!

School Kitchen Tips

- These wraps are a great way to use leftover cooked chicken.
- For more flavour, season the chicken with a mixture of ½ tsp salt, 1 tsp paprika, ½ tsp garlic powder, ½ tsp onion powder, and ½ tsp oregano before baking.

"I like that the cafeteria staff that serve us are really nice. They know the foods I like and how much I like to eat."

Grade 5 student

"The Nova Scotia Lunch Program has created a mealtime family. The recipes are fantastic to work with. All tried and true. Favourites at our school are tacos, pizza, wraps, and pasta dishes. I would like to thank all involved in the creation of this program. If I had to measure our success by the smiles, we would all get an A+."

Melisca, School Food Lead

Did You Know?

Salting meat a day or two before cooking gives it time to absorb the salt, making it more flavourful, tender, and juicy.

PICNIC Plate

MAKES: 4 PLATES* (WITH EXTRA RANCH DIP AND HUMMUS)

*If chicken and hummus are prepared.

Picnic plates are the bee's knees! These Nova Scotia School Lunch Program favourites are filled to overflowing with *ki'kli'kwej* (Mi'kmaw word for chicken), crunchy vegetables, pita wedges, sweet fruit, and two delicious spreads: Ranch Dip and Hummus. You can use store-bought hummus and ranch dip, or try making your own with the simple recipes on the next page.

For a vegetarian Picnic Plate, increase the serving of hummus with each plate or add slices of your favourite cheese.

What You Need

- ½ cucumber
- 1 red pepper
- 1 large carrot
- ¼ honeydew or other melon
- 2 pita breads
- ¾ lb (340 g) cooked chicken, sliced (see recipe pg 37)
- **Ranch Dip** (see recipe)
- **Hummus** (see recipe)

Slice the cucumber into rounds. Seed the pepper and cut it into thin strips. Peel the carrot and cut it into sticks. Slice the melon and the pita breads into wedges. Arrange plates with the cucumber, peppers, carrots, melon, pita wedges, and chicken. Add a big spoonful of Hummus to each plate along with a little dish of Ranch Dressing, for dipping!

RANCH DIP

MAKES ABOUT 2 CUPS (500 ML)

This delicious sauce works well as a salad dressing, a dip, or as a tangy sauce for the Build-Your-Own Chicken Ranch Wraps (see recipe on page 36). If you have fresh herbs, mince them finely and stir them into the dressing to liven up the flavour.

What You Need:

- 1 Tbsp (15 ml) dried parsley or 2 Tbsp (30 ml) chopped fresh parsley
- 1 tsp (5 ml) garlic powder
- 1 tsp (5 ml) onion powder
- 1 tsp (5 ml) dried dill
- ½ tsp (2.5 ml) pepper
- ½ tsp (2.5 ml) salt
- 1 cup (250 ml) mayonnaise
- 1 cup (250 ml) plain yogurt
- 2 tsp (10 ml) white or apple cider vinegar

In a bowl, combine the parsley, garlic powder, onion powder, dill, pepper, salt, mayonnaise, yogurt, and vinegar. Whisk well to combine.

Taste with a carrot stick or lettuce leaf and see if the dressing needs a bit more of anything. Store in the fridge for up to one week.

HUMMUS

MAKES ABOUT 2 CUPS (500 ML)

What You Need

- 1 (540) ml can chickpeas, drained
- 1 small clove garlic, minced
- 3 Tbsp (45 ml) tahini or sunflower butter, optional
- 2 Tbsp (30 ml) lemon juice
- 2 Tbsp (30 ml) water
- ½ tsp (2.5 ml) salt

In a food processor bowl or blender, combine the chickpeas, minced garlic, optional tahini or sunflower butter, lemon juice, water, and salt.

Blend for 5–7 minutes, scraping down the sides from time to time, until the hummus is very smooth. If the mixture seems too dry, add a little water and blend again. Store refrigerated for up to three days.

"Skyla, a Grade 2 student at our school, has been coming to the cafeteria for lunches daily since the lunch program started. When food service workers asked her if she didn't like the lunch she had brought from home, she responded, 'You guys are just such great cookers!' Needless to say, Skyla and her comment certainly made our day! We are loving the School Lunch Program: it is a joy to make sure each and every child is getting a delicious and nutritious meal, even if they did not order it."

Sonya, cafeteria worker

Allergy Alert!

Tahini is made from sesame, a common allergen, so this ingredient is no longer part of the recipe used in schools. Be sure to check if anyone you are cooking for has a sesame allergy.

Corn CHOWDER

MAKES: 12 CUPS

This tasty recipe is based on one originally developed by Rosie Gair and cafeteria staff at the South Shore Regional Centre for Education. Adding carrot or sweet potato to the chowder makes it taste rich and sweet. In the Nova Scotia School Lunch Program the corn chowder is served up with a piece of Lu'skinikn (see recipe on page 42), a truly delicious combination. The Mi'kmaw word for corn chowder is *pie'skmnapu'l* (be-yes-kamn-abool).

What You Need

- 1 large onion
- 1 large carrot or 1 small sweet potato
- 1 lb (454 g) white potatoes
- 2 Tbsp (30 ml) margarine or oil
- ¼ tsp (1.25 ml) nutmeg, optional
- ¼ tsp (1.25 ml) dried thyme, optional
- 1 ½ tsp (7.5 ml) salt
- 3 cups (750 ml) water
- 3 cups (750 ml) milk
- 1 Tbsp (15 ml) cornstarch
- 2 lb (900g) corn, fresh or frozen

School Kitchen Tips

- Corn chowder and other soups freeze well but take a very long time to defrost, up to three days in the refrigerator. Make sure to plan ahead.
- Adding dry cornstarch to hot liquid creates clumps, so always mix it with a bit of cold liquid before adding it to the soup.
- Add extra protein to this chowder by stirring in some haddock or other white fish, salmon, chicken, or cooked beans.

USE IT UP:
You can use leftover mashed pumpkin or squash instead of the carrot or sweet potato and add it with the corn in step 5.

Start Cooking!

1. Peel and mince the onion. Peel the carrot or sweet potato and grate or dice. Peel the white potatoes or scrub very well and dice.

2. Heat the margarine or oil in a large pot over medium-high heat. Add the onions, carrots or sweet potatoes, optional nutmeg, optional dried thyme, and salt. Cook, stirring often, until the onions are tender, about 10–15 minutes.

3. Add the diced white potatoes and water and bring the pot to a boil. Reduce the heat to medium-high and simmer until the potatoes are cooked through, about 15–20 minutes.

4. Mix the cornstarch with ½ cup of the milk and pour the remaining milk into the soup. Stir the cornstarch mixture well and pour it into the soup. Continue to stir and cook until the soup bubbles and thickens.

5. Stir in the corn, taste, and serve. Refrigerate leftovers promptly in a sealed container for up to three days. Freeze for longer storage.

FUN FACTS!

Corn was first cultivated by Indigenous peoples in southern Mexico and Peru and made its way north through Indigenous trade networks. Gaspé Flint corn, a fast-maturing corn that reaches only a few feet high with small cobs, was developed for the short growing season in some areas of Mi'kma'ki.

Many more varieties of flint corn are cultivated by other Indigenous peoples in the Wabanaki Confederacy, including Calais Abenaki, a beautiful corn that grows into shades of golden yellow, maroon, and burnt orange. Flint corn can be eaten while immature much like the sweet corn used in this corn chowder, but it most often is dried for long storage.

LOCAL FOOD FEATURE: CORN

Along with obtaining food through hunting and fishing, a vast array of food plants have been cared for and enjoyed by Mi'kmaq for millenia, including berries, sunflowers, groundnut or wild potato, wild rice, and corn. Many Mi'kmaq are revitalizing traditional growing practices, including cultivating heritage corn varieties.

Flint corn gets its name from the hard, flint-like outer layer that forms on the kernels when dried. Dried flint corn is treated with an alkaline solution to soften the corn and release nutrients. The treated corn can then be ground to make tortillas or cooked into soups. Although sweet corn is now often used in this dish, corn chowder originated from flint corn soups that were prepared by First Nations peoples.

Gaspé Flint corn
Photo credit: Annapolis Seeds

Four Sisters

Indigenous agricultural practices across Turtle Island (North America) include growing corn together with other plants like squash and beans, known as the Three Sisters. A staff member at Nourish Nova Scotia shares that he learned about a fourth Sister, the sunflower, from a Mi'kmaw Elder.

The plants help one another to grow: *Pie'skmn* (corn) stands tall, giving **beans** something to climb up. ***Wikunn* (beans)** help out too—they put special nutrients into the soil to keep it healthy. ***Ejkuj* (squash)** spreads its big leaves over the ground, stopping pesky weeds and keeping the soil moist. ***Wasuek* (sunflowers)** protect the other plants from strong winds and attract bees to help pollinate them.

LU'SKINIKN

MAKES: 12 PIECES

Lu'skinikn (loo-skin-e-gen), often shortened to *lu'ski*, is a delicious quickbread similar in texture to a tea biscuit. This bread became a necessary staple in Mi'kmaw communities after colonization, as Indigenous people were moved onto reserves, unable to hunt and fish, and supplied with rations which included flour.

This recipe is adapted from one of several recipes you can find on the *Nilu'nal* app and was contributed by Elder Joanne Cope. Developed by Mi'kmaw Kina'matnewey, the Nilu'nal app also includes recipes for Eel Soup, Baked Beans, and Moose Roast.

What You Need

- Oil, for greasing the pan
- 5 cups (600 g) all-purpose flour
- ¼ cup (60 ml) baking powder
- 1 tsp salt
- ½ cup oil
- 2 cups (500 ml) water

Start Cooking!

1. Preheat the oven to 350°F and grease a 9" x 13" baking pan or line with parchment paper. In a bowl, combine flour, baking powder, and salt.
2. Add the oil and water and stir until the dough is evenly moistened. Knead the dough with clean hands until it is smooth, then pat it evenly into the pan.
3. Use a knife to score (cut halfway through) the dough into the desired number of squares. Bake for 25–30 minutes, until golden brown. Cut pieces all the way through and serve.

School Kitchen Tip

- Though not traditional, you can make Lu'skinikn with half whole wheat flour or all whole wheat flour.

Did You Know?

Lu'skinikn is also called Four Cents Cake, especially around Unamak'i (Cape Breton) because the ingredients used to make it cost 4 cents in the past. There is also a version called Fry Bread, made with a similar dough, and fried in hot fat.

If you would like to cook along with an adorable bear cub, search online for the video *"Aliet Learns to Make Lu'skinikn"* from Mi'kmaw Kina'matnewey and Sprig Learning.

Today! Harvest
NOURISH TRAILER
SHED

Chicken SHAWARMA

MAKES: 4 WRAPS

Chicken Shawarma originated in the Levant region. Lebanese Canadian restaurant owners like the Nahas, who founded the Mezza restaurant franchise, introduced shawarma to Nova Scotia in the 1990s. Marinated chicken is slow-roasted on a vertical spit, and traditionally served with *toum*, a garlic sauce. This is a simplified recipe that is great for home cooking. For a twist, serve the spiced chicken and toppings over rice as a Shawarma Bowl!

What You Need

FOR THE WRAPS

- 4 whole wheat pitas or tortillas

FOR THE SPICE MIX

- ½ tsp (2.5 ml) salt
- 1 tsp (5 ml) ground cumin
- ½ tsp (2.5 ml) ground coriander
- ½ tsp (2.5 ml) turmeric
- ½ tsp (2.5 ml) paprika
- ¼ tsp (1.25 ml) cinnamon

FOR THE CHICKEN

- 1 lb (454 g) boneless, skinless chicken thighs or breasts
- 1 ½ tsp (7.5 ml) white or apple cider vinegar
- 1 Tbsp (15 ml) oil

FOR THE SAUCE

- ½ cup (125 ml) mayonnaise
- 1 minced garlic clove or 1 tsp (5 ml) garlic powder
- 1 Tbsp (15 ml) lemon juice or white vinegar

YOUR CHOICE OF TOPPINGS

diced tomato, sliced onion, grated carrot, diced cucumber, shredded lettuce, fried potatoes, roasted sweet potatoes, sliced cucumber pickles, pickled turnip, harissa

FUN FACTS!

Like tomatoes, cucumbers are actually fruits, not vegetables.

"Cool as a cucumber" is more than just a saying. The inside of a cucumber can be as much as 8 degrees cooler than the air around it!

Start Cooking!

1 **For the spice mix**, combine the salt, cumin, coriander, turmeric, paprika, and cinnamon.

2 **To prepare the chicken**, cut it into thin strips and add the vinegar, and spice mix. Toss to combine thoroughly. If you have time, cover the bowl and refrigerate for at least an hour, or overnight if possible.

3 Make the sauce by whisking the mayonnaise, garlic or garlic powder, and lemon juice or vinegar. **Prepare the toppings** you would like to serve.

4 To cook the chicken, heat a large frying pan on medium heat. Add the oil and carefully swirl it around the pan. Cook and stir the chicken until golden brown and no longer pink inside when you carefully cut into a piece, about 8–10 minutes.

5 Warm the pitas or tortillas up by microwaving for a few seconds or toasting in a toaster oven for 1 minute. Top each wrap with the chicken, sauce, and chosen toppings. Roll tightly and enjoy!

6 Refrigerate leftovers promptly. Leftover Chicken Shawarma will keep for up to three days in the refrigerator.

LOCAL FOOD FEATURE: CUCUMBERS

Crispy and cool cucumbers are often served in the school lunch program. Several farms in Nova Scotia grow cucumbers, often in greenhouses to extend the growing season. The largest of these is **den Haan Greenhouses** in Annapolis County. Dutch immigrants Helena and Jac den Haan immigrated to Nova Scotia in 1951 with thirteen children. Starting with just one greenhouse, they have expanded through the years. Now, the third generation of den Haans grow cucumbers and mini-cucumbers in eight acres of indoor growing space. If you drive by the greenhouses at night, you will see the bright pink glow in the sky from the LED grow lights they use to grow cucumbers year-round.

Baby cucumbers in the pink glow of den Haan's grow lights

Photo credit: Jodi den Haan

School Kitchen Tip

- Instead of frying, the seasoned chicken can be spread on a greased 8″ x 8″ pan and baked at 350°F for 15-20 minutes until cooked through and no longer pink inside when cut.

"I think the lunch program is going really well! A lot of my friends didn't used to eat lunch, either because they didn't want to pack something or they didn't want to eat at school, but now we all order lunch and eat together."

Sophie, Grade 8 student

School Food Hero

Photo credit: Hela Soubgui

Hela with her family

Hela Soubgui, a caterer from the sunny seaside town of Monastir, Tunisia, shared the shawarma recipe used in the first year of the Nova Scotia School Lunch Program. After moving to Nova Scotia in 2020, she launched **Easy Peasy Tunisian Cuisine** at the New Glasgow Farmers' Market. Now at the Wolfville Farmers' Market, she serves favourites like couscous with dill, baklava, and shawarma. To recreate her shawarma, use this spice mix: 2 tsp garlic powder, 1 tsp onion powder, ⅛ tsp ground cloves, ¼ tsp black pepper, and 1 tsp paprika.

FISH CAKES
& Quick Baked Beans

MAKES: 16 FISH CAKES & SMALL POT OF BEANS

A tasty Maritime staple for centuries, fish cakes have long held a special place at the African Nova Scotian table. Salt cod is traditional in African Nova Scotian communities, but you can also use leftover cooked fish. Fish cakes are especially delicious when cooked until crispy and golden-brown, and go well with a variety of side dishes like salads, baked beans, cornbread, and pickles.

Please note: salt cod should be soaked the day before making fish cakes for the best results.

Recipe contributor Wendie Wilson suggests dusting the fish cakes with flour seasoned with salt and pepper before frying.

What You Need:

FOR THE FISH CAKES

- 1 lb (454g) salt cod or other salted white fish
- 2 lb (900 g, about 2 large) potatoes
- 1 medium onion
- 2 tsp (10 ml) summer savory
- ¼ cup (60 ml) oil

FOR THE QUICK BAKED BEANS

- 1 (540 ml) can navy beans
- ½ cup (125 ml) water
- 1 tsp (5 ml) mustard powder or prepared mustard
- 2 Tbsp (30 ml) brown sugar
- 1 Tbsp (15 ml) molasses
- ½ tsp (2.5 ml) salt
- Pinch of black pepper
- 1 small onion, diced, or 1 tsp onion powder

TO SERVE: Tartar sauce, ketchup, or relish like chow chow, coleslaw or other salad, cooked veggies, cornbread, fruit

"The fish cakes? I really like them! I like them a lot! I like almost everything in the lunch program. I usually get second servings."
Grade 5 student

Did You Know?

Yellow-eyed beans are traditionally used for making baked beans in African Nova Scotian cooking. You can find recipes for authentic slow-cooked beans online and in Nova Scotian cookbooks like *In the Africville Kitchen: The Comforts of Home.*

Start Cooking!

1 **To make the fish cakes,** place the salt fish in a bowl or container and add cold water to cover. Allow the fish to soak overnight in the refrigerator. The next day, drain the fish and place in a pot with enough fresh water to cover. Bring to a boil and immediately turn off the heat. Drain the fish well and let cool.

2 Peel and dice the potatoes and finely mince the onion. Place the potatoes in a pot and add enough water to cover. Over high heat, bring the potatoes to a boil. Reduce the heat to medium-high and cook until tender, about 10–15 minutes.

3 Carefully drain the potatoes, then return them to the pot and mash well. Add the flaked fish to the pot with the potatoes along with the minced onion and summer savory. Mix well with clean hands to combine, then shape the mixture into round patties roughly 3 inches in diameter. It helps to wet your hands from time to time while you do this.

4 **To make the baked beans,** empty the navy beans into a small pot with their liquid. Add the water, mustard powder, brown sugar, molasses, salt, black pepper, and onion. Bring to a boil, then reduce to a simmer and cook until the sauce has thickened, about 30 minutes.

5 Heat a heavy frying pan over medium heat and add enough oil to generously coat the bottom. Cook the fish cakes in batches, adding oil as necessary until golden brown and cooked through.

6 Serve the crispy fish cakes with the beans and any toppings you like. Refrigerate leftovers promptly. Leftover fish cakes and baked beans can be stored for up to three days in the refrigerator. Freeze for longer storage.

Did You Know?

John Hodge, an African American chemist, made discoveries about the chemical reactions that take place during the browning process of cooked foods. Though the term for this process, the Maillard reaction, is named after the scientist who first discovered it, John Hodge's research has led to a deeper understanding of how this process makes foods like bread, grilled meat, and chocolate so delicious!

African Nova Scotian Food Artwork by Wendie Wilson

School Food Hero

Wendie Wilson is a cultural advocate, artist, author, and educator who has devoted her life to celebrating African Nova Scotian heritage. Wendie grew up in Uniacke Square, where she walked home every day for lunch, enjoying foods grown and prepared by her family.

Wendie's aunt Edith Chandler was a founding member of the Hot Lunch program known as the "Dinner Church" at New Horizons Baptist Church. For over 30 years, program lead Evelina Upshaw led a group of cooks in preparing and serving a free lunch to children in Uniacke Square. Such programs led by African Nova Scotian communities have inspired folks around Nova Scotia to this day.

Wendie promotes the vast African Nova Scotian repertoire of culinary traditions, taking part in advocacy groups including the Pan-African Canadian Food Sovereignty Network.

Chicken Noodle STIR FRY with Vegetables

MAKES: 4–6 BOWLS

This recipe is a simple version of Chow Mein, or fried noodles, a beloved Chinese Canadian dish. You can substitute 1 lb boneless pork cut into thin strips, or ground chicken or pork, for the boneless chicken in this recipe. For a vegetarian version, swap in 1 lb tofu, crumbled or cubed, for the chicken.

FUN FACTS!

Broccoli is made up of lots of tiny flower buds called "florets."

Most of the broccoli grown in Nova Scotia comes from the Annapolis Valley.

What You Need

FOR THE CHICKEN AND VEGETABLES

- ½ head broccoli
- 1 bell pepper, any colour
- 1 large or 2 medium carrots
- 1 lb (454 g) boneless, skinless chicken breast or thighs

FOR THE SAUCE

- 2–3 cloves garlic
- 1 tsp (5 ml) grated fresh ginger or ginger powder
- 2 Tbsp (30 ml) oil
- ½ cup (125 ml) water
- ½ cup (125 ml) soy sauce, lower sodium if possible
- 3 Tbsp (45 ml) brown sugar or honey
- 1 Tbsp (15 ml) white or apple cider vinegar
- 1 Tbsp (15 ml) cornstarch

FOR THE NOODLES

- 2 tsp (10 ml) salt
- 1 (340 g) pkg spaghetti or noodles of your choice

TO COOK

- 2 Tbsp (30 ml) oil

USE IT UP

Don't forget to include the stem of the broccoli. Trim off the end of the stem, then carefully use a peeler to remove any tough skin. Cut the stem into thin pieces and cook along with the florets.

Start Cooking!

1. **For the chicken and vegetables,** cut the broccoli florets from the main stem, and slice any large pieces into smaller ones (see tip for using the stem on page 48). Cut the pepper into thin strips. Peel the carrots and grate them.

2. Slice the chicken into thin strips, then place them in a bowl. Thoroughly wash the cutting board.

3. **To make the sauce,** mince the garlic and combine with the ginger powder, oil, water, soy sauce, brown sugar or honey, vinegar, and cornstarch in a jar or measuring cup. Mix well.

4. **Cook the noodles.** Bring a large pot to a boil over high heat. Add the salt and spaghetti. Stir well, then cook the noodles until tender, stirring from time to time. Drain and return to the pot to keep warm.

5. Heat a frying pan or wok over medium-high heat and add 1 Tbsp oil and the broccoli. Cook and stir the broccoli until bright green and crisp-tender. Add the broccoli to the noodles along with the carrots and peppers.

6. Return the pan or wok to the heat and add 1 Tbsp oil. Cook and stir the chicken until golden brown and no longer pink inside when you carefully cut into a piece, about 8–10 minutes.

7. Add the noodle and vegetable mixture to the pan with the chicken. Give the sauce a final stir to make sure it is well mixed, then add it to the pan. Stir and cook until the sauce bubbles and thickens and everything is well combined.

8. Leftovers can be refrigerated for up to three days and taste delicious straight from the fridge.

LOCAL FOOD FEATURE: BROCCOLI

On the rolling hills of Delhaven in the Annapolis Valley, **Randsland Farms** grow five varieties of broccoli, along with kale and cabbage. Nowadays, broccoli is a very popular vegetable, but it hasn't always been available in Nova Scotia. In fact, the Rand family helped to introduce it to Nova Scotians in the 1980s!

School Kitchen Tips

- If you have fresh ginger, use about 2 tsp (10 ml) grated or minced ginger in place of the ginger powder.
- Sliced mushrooms, shredded cabbage, snow peas, green onions, and bean sprouts are all delicious additions to this dish. Stir-fry them along with the broccoli.

"None of this would be possible without the dedication and passion of our food service staff. They have shown a true commitment to their school communities and students, taking pride in providing healthy, delicious, and appealing meals every day. Their hard work and care are making a real difference in the lives of the students they serve."

Carrie, School Food Lead

School Food Heroes

The original Chicken Noodle Stir Fry recipe that launched the Lunch Program was co-developed with Indira Persaud and Chris Wong. Chris and his wife, Candy, are the owners of Gold Medal Restaurant in Salisbury, New Brunswick. Indira is a Red Seal Chef who leads a team of four cafeteria staff at Kings County Academy, where they regularly feed up to 400 students every day.

Their recipe is one of 23 in Nourish Nova Scotia's Local Food Lunch Toolkit. Find it at: *nourishns.ca/resource/local-food-lunch-toolkit-for-food-service-providers*

MAC & CHEESE

MAKES: 4–6 BOWLS

James Hemings, the first African American chef trained in France, is credited with introducing macaroni and cheese to the United States in the late 18th century. Chef Hemings likely thickened the sauce with a mix of butter and flour known as a *roux*, just like in this recipe. You can make your Mac and Cheese extra special by setting out a few fun toppings so that everyone can make it their way.

What You Need

FOR THE SAUCE

- 2 cups (225 g) grated cheddar cheese
- ¼ cup (60 ml) margarine
- ¼ cup all-purpose flour
- 2 cups (500 ml) milk
- 2 Tbsp (30 ml) Parmesan cheese
- ½ tsp (2.5 ml) salt
- ½ tsp (2.5 ml) mustard powder, optional
- 1 cup (250 ml) mashed sweet potato or squash, optional

FOR THE PASTA

- 1 (340–454 g) pkg macaroni or other pasta, whole wheat if you like
- 1 Tbsp (15 ml) salt

YOUR CHOICE OF TOPPINGS

cooked lean ground beef, leftover chili, flaked tuna, diced chicken, chopped tomatoes or cherry tomatoes, cooked broccoli or cauliflower, peas, cooked spinach or kale, sliced green onions, crispy bread crumbs, hot sauce, ketchup

Start Cooking!

1. **To make the sauce**, grate the cheese if needed. Melt the margarine over medium-low heat in a medium sized pot, preferably with a heavy bottom. Whisk in the flour and cook for 1 minute. Slowly add the milk, whisking constantly to avoid lumps. Continue to whisk frequently as the mixture thickens and begins to bubble, about 5–10 minutes. Remove from heat.

2. Sprinkle in the cheddar and Parmesan cheeses, salt, optional mustard powder and optional mashed sweet potato or squash. Whisk well to combine. Taste and add a pinch more salt if necessary.

3. Meanwhile, bring a large pot of water to a boil. Add the macaroni and salt and boil until the macaroni is tender, about 10 minutes. Carefully drain the macaroni, then return it to the cooking pot. Pour in the cheese sauce and stir to combine. Serve with toppings of your choice.

4. Leftover mac and cheese can be refrigerated for up to three days.

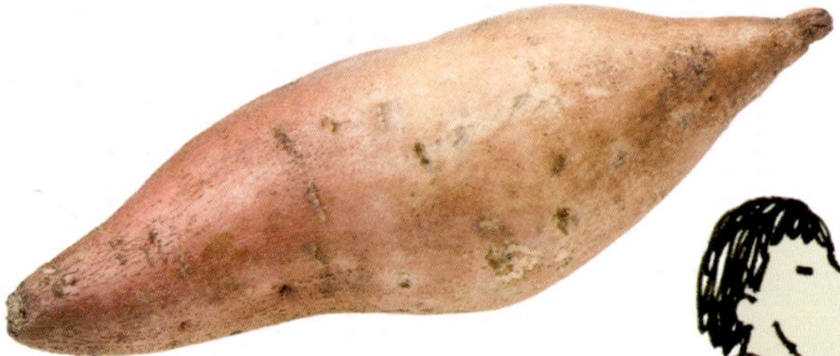

"I loved the subtle flavour of Parmesan in the sauce and the bright orange colour."

Rachel, Grade 10

FUN FACTS!

Sweet potatoes can be orange, yellow, red, white, or purple.

Sweet potatoes are delicious whether they're boiled, roasted, baked, microwaved, fried, or grilled. Sweet potatoes can also be eaten raw.

LOCAL FOOD FEATURE: SWEET POTATOES

Valley Harvest Sweet Potatoes is owned by the Keddy family in Lakeville, Kings County. With help from an expert team of employees from the Annapolis Valley, Jamaica, and Mexico, they grow and harvest over 1 million pounds of sweet potatoes each year. The school-aged generation of Keddys grow strawberries and pumpkins to sell at their roadside stand. Some of their favourite Nova Scotia School Lunch Program meals include the Chicken Ranch Wrap, Corn Chowder with Lu'skinikn, and Mac and Cheese.

Photo credit: Katie Keddy

Phil Keddy checks in on baby sweet potatoes in the field. The Keddys have grown sweet potatoes that weigh as much as 10 pounds!

PASTA with Tomato Beef Sauce

MAKES: 4–6 PLATES

Around the mid-1800s an Italian settlement began to grow in Cape Breton. By 1921 there were over one thousand Italian people living in and around Sydney, New Waterford, and Glace Bay. They brought cherished food traditions to their new life in Nova Scotia, introducing tasty dishes like *porchetta* (slow-roasted pork), pizza, and pasta with tomato sauce. This simple and zesty tomato beef sauce is a lunchtime favourite and can be served with any pasta!

What You Need

FOR THE SAUCE

- 1 medium onion
- ¼ lb (125 g) mushrooms
- 3 cloves garlic or 1 Tbsp (15 ml) garlic powder
- 1 large carrot
- 1 Tbsp (15 ml) oil
- 1 lb (454 g) lean ground beef
- 1 (798 ml) can crushed tomatoes or whole tomatoes, blended until smooth
- 1 (156 ml) can tomato paste
- 1 Tbsp (15 ml) sugar, or to taste
- 1 ½ tsp (7.5 ml) dried oregano
- 1 Tbsp (15 ml) dried basil
- ¾ tsp (3 ml) salt
- 2 cups (500 ml) water

FOR THE PASTA

- 1 (340–454 g) pkg fusilli, penne, or spaghetti, whole wheat if you like
- 2 Tbsp (30 ml) salt

TO SERVE: grated Parmesan cheese

FUN FACT!

Wenjitia'm (wen-jew-dee-yah-m) is the Mik'maq word for cow, and translates to "French moose."

School Kitchen Tips

- To make a vegetarian tomato pasta sauce, substitute 1 (540 ml) can of lentils for the ground beef and add it in step 2. You may also enjoy this with half ground beef and half lentils.
- If you are using whole wheat pasta, it tastes best when it is fully cooked.

Start Cooking!

1. **For the sauce**, peel and dice the onion. Mince the mushrooms and garlic if using. Peel the carrot and mince or grate it.

2. Pour the oil into a large heavy-bottomed pot on medium heat. Add the ground beef, onions, mushrooms, carrot, and garlic. Cook, stirring often, until the beef has browned and the vegetables are soft and golden brown, about 15 minutes.

3. Add the crushed tomatoes, tomato paste, sugar, oregano, basil, ¾ tsp salt, and water. Reduce the heat to low and simmer for about 30 minutes, or until the sauce has thickened. Keep warm over low heat, adding water to thin if necessary.

4. **Cook the pasta.** Bring a large pot of water to a boil and add 2 Tbsp salt. Add the pasta, stirring to make sure the pasta doesn't stick together. Boil for the time indicated on the package or until tender, then drain. Combine the pasta with the sauce or serve the pasta and sauce separately. Top each serving with a spoonful of Parmesan cheese.

5. Refrigerate leftovers promptly. Leftover pasta and sauce can be stored in the refrigerator for up to three days or frozen for longer storage.

"One of the most memorable moments I've seen was at Islands Consolidated, where students were able to come together in the cafeteria for lunch for the first time in years. Previously, they didn't have a stable lunch program, and meals were often eaten in classrooms. Seeing the excitement on their faces as they lined up for a hot meal and sat with their friends was truly special—the energy was electric, and the smiles were endless."

Carrie, School Food Lead

Handmade PIZZA

MAKES: 12 SLICES

Pizza is on every Nova Scotia School Food Program menu, but it looks different at each school–some use pita bread, some use dough, and others use English muffins. No matter the style, pizza is the most-loved meal on the menu.

This recipe makes pizza from scratch, including an easy no-knead dough and sauce. Short on time? Use English muffins or pita bread instead. The sauce makes enough for four pizzas and freezes well. No carrots? Swap in diced zucchini, peppers, mushrooms, or even apples!

Nutrition Bites

Whole wheat flour is a great way to add extra flavour and nutrition to your baking. It's packed with fibre and can add a delicious nutty taste to your recipes. If you want to give it a try, start by mixing half whole wheat with half white flour to find what you like best.

What You Need

FOR THE DOUGH

- 1 ½ cups (375 ml) warm water
- 1 Tbsp (15 ml) yeast
- 1 ½ cups (375 ml) all-purpose flour
- 1 ½ cups (375 ml) whole wheat flour
- 1 tsp (5 ml) salt
- 1 Tbsp (15 ml) oil, plus more for greasing the pan

FOR THE SAUCE

- 1 large onion
- 2 large carrots
- 4 cloves garlic or 2 tsp (10 ml) garlic powder
- 2 Tbsp (30 ml) oil
- 1 Tbsp (15 ml) dried oregano
- 2 tsp (10 ml) salt
- 1 (540 ml) can crushed tomatoes
- 2 tsp (10 ml) sugar, optional (if the tomatoes are quite tart)

TO ASSEMBLE THE PIZZA

- 1 Tbsp (15 ml) oil
- 2 ½ cups (300 g) shredded mozzarella

YOUR CHOICE OF TOPPINGS

cooked lean ground beef, diced peppers, sliced mushrooms, diced onions, sliced olives, diced tomatoes, diced pineapple, baby spinach

"I'm excited when it's something I really like. The one that is my really favourite is the pizza!"

Grade 2 student

Start Cooking!

1. **To make the dough**, pour the warm water into a large bowl and sprinkle in the yeast. After 5 minutes, add the all-purpose flour, whole wheat flour, and 1 tsp salt. Stir with a large spoon for 2 minutes, or until all the flour is incorporated. The dough will be very sticky and your spoon will be a mess! Scrape off the spoon and drizzle the dough with 1 Tbsp of oil.

2. Cover the bowl and let the dough rise in a warm place until it is twice as big as when you mixed it, 45 minutes to 1 hour. While the dough rises, make your pizza sauce.

3. **To make the sauce**, peel the onion and dice. Peel and mince the carrots and garlic. Heat the oil over medium-low heat in a heavy-bottomed pot and add the onion, carrot, and garlic. Cook until the vegetables are well-softened and just beginning to brown, about 15 minutes.

4. Add the oregano and 2 tsp salt and stir for another minute, then add the crushed tomatoes.

5. Simmer for at least 10 minutes, then taste and decide if a little sugar is needed to balance the tartness of the tomatoes. Cool the sauce slightly and blend with an immersion blender if a very smooth sauce is desired. You will only need 1 ½ cups for this recipe, and the remaining sauce can be frozen in 1 ½ cup batches.

6. Preheat the oven to 400°F. Line a baking sheet with parchment paper if you have it. Grease the pan with 1 Tbsp oil. Gently ease the dough onto the centre of the pan. Wash your hands, then pour a little oil onto them so they don't stick to the dough. Gently spread the dough into a large oval. Let the dough rest for at least 5 minutes, then evenly push the dough to fill the pan.

7. Top the dough with 1 ½ cups of the pizza sauce and spread it out evenly on the dough. Add the toppings and sprinkle with the shredded mozzarella. Bake the pizza for 15–20 minutes, until the crust is browned and the cheese is bubbling and beginning to brown.

8. Carefully remove the pizza from the oven using oven mitts and place on a heatproof surface. Let cool for a few minutes, then carefully cut it into serving pieces using a pizza cutter or sharp knife. Store any leftovers in the refrigerator for up to three days.

School Kitchen Tips

- If you don't have whole wheat flour, use 3 cups (750 ml) total all-purpose flour.
- If your dough refuses to stretch, give it a few minutes to relax before pushing it out evenly into the pan.
- You can swap in 6 pitas or English muffins for the dough. Spread with sauce, add toppings and cheese, and bake until the cheese is beginning to brown, 10–12 minutes.

School Food Story

Sixty years ago, pizza was unfamiliar to most Nova Scotians. In the 1960s, brothers George and Jim Kouyas opened Sam's Pizza in Stellarton after working in Italian pizzerias in Montreal. They created the famous "Pictou County Pizza" brown sauce and brought pizza to the region. The brothers moved to Stellarton to be near the ocean and introduce their recipe. At first, locals were unsure about pizza, but they quickly grew to love it.

These days George's children Spyro, Yota, and Maria run the restaurant and are feeding a new generation of pizza lovers. Maria's son loves the Nova Scotia School Lunch Program pizza. As the third generation in a family of pizza experts, we think that's pretty great!

Photo credit: Sam's Pizza

Did You Know?

Sam's original combo pizza is topped with their famous brown pizza sauce, Brothers pepperoni, mushrooms, peppers, and plenty of cheese!

Butter CHICKEN

MAKES: 4–6 BOWLS

This classic creamy curry, developed with recipe contributor Vijay Luxmi Maharaj, has been a huge hit with students. Sweet potatoes add an extra boost of locally grown flavour. To make a delicious vegetarian dish, substitute 2 (540 ml) cans of drained chickpeas for the chicken. Half chicken and half chickpeas is also delicious—try it and see what you think. If you're serving this dish with rice, remember to start it before you make the Butter Chicken!

What You Need

FOR THE CHICKEN AND VEGETABLES

- 2 lb (900 g) boneless, skinless chicken breast or thighs
- 2 large or 3 medium sweet potatoes
- 1 Tbsp (15 ml) oil

FOR THE SAUCE

- 1 small onion
- 3 cloves garlic or 2 tsp (10 ml) garlic powder
- 1 tsp (5 ml) salt
- 2 tsp (10 ml) paprika
- 2 tsp (10 ml) turmeric
- 1 tsp (5 ml) ground cumin
- 1 tsp (5 ml) ground coriander
- 2 tsp (10 ml) garam masala
- ½ cup (125 ml) water
- 2 Tbsp (30 ml) oil
- 1 ¾ cup (400 ml) canned crushed tomatoes (about half a 798 ml can)
- 1 cup (250 ml) whipping cream or coffee cream (18% milk fat)

SIDES AND TOPPINGS OF YOUR CHOICE: cooked rice, naan or other flatbread, cucumber slices or other veggies, chutney, chopped cilantro

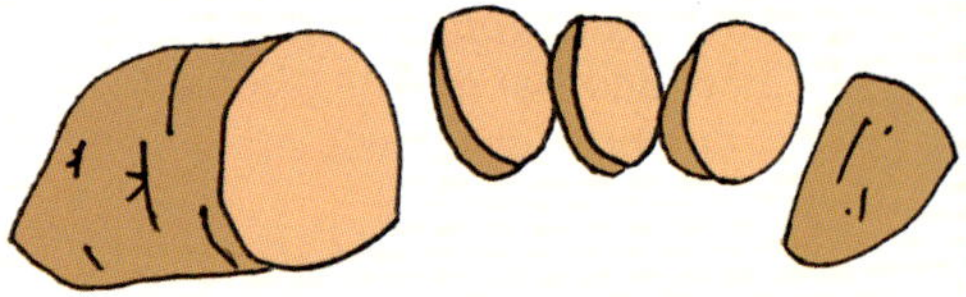

Did You Know?

Every day that Butter Chicken is served, Nova Scotian students eat about 4,000 pounds of sweet potatoes, 5,000 pounds of chicken, and 4,000 cucumbers!

Start Cooking!

1. Cut the chicken into bite-sized pieces. Peel and dice the sweet potatoes.

2. Heat 1 Tbsp oil in a large heavy-bottomed pot over medium-high heat. Add the chicken pieces. Cook and stir the chicken until golden brown and no longer pink inside when you cut into a piece, about 8–10 minutes. Carefully remove the chicken from the pot and set aside.

3. **Make the sauce** while the chicken cooks. Peel and mince the onion and the garlic if using fresh. Mix the garlic powder (if using), salt, paprika, turmeric, cumin, coriander, and garam masala with the water in a small bowl.

4. Place the pot back on the burner over low heat. Add 2 Tbsp oil, onions, and minced garlic if using. Cook and stir for 2–3 minutes, until the onions are beginning to soften. Pour in the spice mix and cook until the water has evaporated and the oil starts to glisten on the surface, about 5 minutes.

5. Add the tomatoes, cream, and sweet potatoes and increase the heat to medium-high. Bring the sauce to a boil, then reduce the heat to medium-low and continue to cook, stirring once in a while, until the sweet potatoes are tender. Add the cooked chicken along with any juices in the bowl.

6. Serve Butter Chicken with rice or naan or other flatbread and the toppings of your choice. Refrigerate leftovers promptly and store for up to three days or freeze for longer storage.

USE IT UP
Freeze the remaining crushed tomatoes for next time, or double the sauce and freeze the extra to make your next batch of Butter Chicken a snap to prepare.

School Kitchen Tips

- Buying spices in bulk makes them much more affordable. Try mixing up a double batch of the spice mix and storing it in a sealed bag or jar for the next time you're craving Butter Chicken.
- Garam masala is a mixture of savoury and sweet spices. If you can't find it at the grocery store, try adding 1 extra tsp cumin, ¼ tsp cinnamon, and a pinch of cloves and nutmeg.
- Leftover cooked, diced chicken works well in this meal. Add it to the simmering sauce once the sweet potatoes are tender. You can also add any leftover veggies that need using up.

"What's truly special is the variety of foods offered. Many of our students are trying fruits, vegetables, and dishes they might not have otherwise had the chance to experience. It's opening their eyes to new tastes and encouraging healthier eating habits that will benefit them for years to come."

Leanne, Principal

School Food Hero

Vijay enjoying tamarind, one of her favourite childhood treats!

Vijay Luxmi Maharaj grew up in Jaipur, India, and moved to Canada in 1991 to work at her family's restaurant. She now runs **Taj Mahal Catering** and is a regular vendor at the Wolfville Farmers' Market, where she serves her famous samosas, pakoras, channa masala, and butter chicken. Vijay kindly shared her Butter Chicken recipe so that students in Nova Scotia can enjoy it too.

Learn More About NOURISH NOVA SCOTIA

At Nourish Nova Scotia, we believe youth are the future—and the foundation for building healthy generations to come. Every young person deserves to be well-nourished and to learn about food in meaningful, engaging ways. That's why we support youth in exploring food and equip them to help shape the food systems around them.

From our early leadership in developing breakfast programs across Nova Scotia, we've played a key role in strengthening and advocating for school food initiatives. Today, we collaborate with schools and communities to improve access to nutritious food, create fun and welcoming spaces where kids can enjoy meals together, and support young leaders who want to take action and make food systems better.

While we don't operate the School Lunch program, we work closely with the Province of Nova Scotia to highlight why school food matters—and how everyone can play a part. We also create opportunities for students to learn about food, get involved, and share their experiences through creative storytelling.

When young people have access to healthy food–and the opportunity to influence the food systems around them–they can become leaders who inspire meaningful change. Empowering that change is at the heart of our work at Nourish Nova Scotia. And if you're reading this, you're already part of it. Thank you for joining us.

In Good Food and Friendship,

Aimee Gasparetto
Executive Director

Nourish
Nova Scotia

Nourish staff in the garden.

Hello friends,

Since I came to work with Nourish Nova Scotia, it has been my dream to help make a family cookbook. And here it is, a collection of recipes and stories from so many amazing people across our province!

My love for recipes began as a child, filling a little box with handwritten cards of recipes from magazines and my mom's cookbook collection. Cooking felt magical—I could recreate favourites, explore new flavours, and bring back special memories. That passion led me to thirty years in foodservice, including running a restaurant with my sister, my mom, and one of my aunts.

My three children grew up in that restaurant, and they taught me so much about cooking with young people. It's also where I got my start in writing and sharing recipes.

When my son was in Grade 8, I was invited to help out in his school kitchen, working with an incredible team to create meals students loved. We started with a salad bar, then developed big- batch recipes for favourites like tacos, burgers, pasta, and treasured dishes shared by local families. The excitement of the students inspired me to share these recipes with other schools and regions. I even got to work with the cafeteria staff in the kitchen of my old high school!

When I came to work with Nourish Nova Scotia, the recipe collection grew. Today, the Nova Scotia School Lunch Program brings some of these recipes to school cafeterias across the province.

Thinking about the many hands preparing school meals each day fills me with gratitude. I hope this cookbook brings you joy as you cook and share food with loved ones!

Jenny Osburn, Nourish staff

About the Illustrator

Photo credit: Kim Campbell Sullivan

Emma FitzGerald was born to Irish parents in Lesotho, a small mountainous kingdom in Southern Africa, and did most of her growing up in Vancouver, BC. These early travels have instilled in her a deep interest in people and places. Following a career path that is part architecture, part art, she received a BFA in visual art from UBC, and a MArch. from Dalhousie School of Architecture. She loves to draw with kids as they are always full of surprises and share their unique ideas. Emma is the author of *Hand Drawn Halifax* (Formac Publishing, 2015) and lives in Lunenburg, Nova Scotia.

Find out more at *emmafitzgerald.ca*

ACKNOWLEDGMENTS

Nourish Nova Scotia would like to thank everyone who contributed to the making of this cookbook!

We have noted where many of the recipes in this book originated, but we recognize that many people have collaborated to make these recipes the best they can be and that we haven't even come close to naming them all. Thank you!

Special thanks to our recipe testers, who tasted their way through every dish with care and enthusiasm: Kim, Jill, Ava, Siena, Aimee, Lindsay, Lori, Claire, Raina, Rachel, Liam, Lori, Gabe, Liv, Annette, Meagan, Rachel, Kris, Rory, Ami, Ana; Paige, Laceigh, Octavia, Eris, Valerie, and Olivia at Dove Program Cape Breton; Kendra and participants at Our House Youth Wellness Centre, and Nichole and Grade 10 students at West Kings High School!

Thank you to our contributors and advisors: Chelsey Purdy, Hela Soubgui, Paul Heighton, Wendie Wilson, Jordan Eyamie, Rosie Gair, Indira Persaud, Gary Dunfield, Shaun Zwarun, Paul Thimot, Evelyn Ernst, Chris and Candy Wong, Valerie Mansour, Joanne Cope, Maria Walsh, Vijay Luxmi Maharaj, Kielyn Jenkins, Whitney Moran, Scott Olszowiec, Terrilee Bulger, Sherie Hodds, Andy Hay, Christine Riordan, Lisa Dexter, Arlene Drew, Kris Gaudet, Sophie Mathieu-Gauthier, Missy Searle, Hilary Briar, Karen Provo, Barb Lipp, Cynthia Bazinet, Phil and Katie Keddy, Jodi den Haan, Sarah Mullen, April MacLean, Amelia Reid, Katrina Sokolowski, Alex Burke, Amanda Northcott, Marc Deveau, Kyla Pierik, Paula Putnam, Efren Delgado, Brad Keddy, Donna Allan, and all of the committed staff and board members at Nourish Nova Scotia—past and present.

Thank you to our distribution partners at The Flower Cart, and to Nimbus Publishing!

***Wela'lin*, thank you, to Marilyn Francis for sharing the Mi'kmaw language used in this book.**

Most of all, we thank the caring folks in every corner of Nova Scotia working to feed our children quality meals, made from scratch, with love and creativity.

Food photo credits: Lia Chin-Yet (pg 4-24, 50, 54); Province of Nova Scotia (pg 26, 28, 32-46, 52, 58); Jenny Osburn (pg 30, 48)

FURTHER READING:

Chop Suey Nation Anhua Xu

L'Nu'k: The People Theresa Meuse

Mitji—Let's Eat! Margaret Augustine and Lauren Beck

Pantry and Palate Simon Thibault

In the Africville Kitchen Juanita Peters, Claudia Castillo-Prentt, and Adina Fraser-Marsman

Nature's Grocery Store Wendie Wilson

Italian Lives, Cape Breton Memories Sam Migliore and A. Evo Dipierro

Out of Old Nova Scotia Kitchens Marie Nightingale

Emma FitzGerald led workshops with Heather Docherty and Macy Shea's Grade 6 classes at Oxford School in Halifax. Their work is featured on pages 7 and 63 of this cookbook. We appreciate their enthusiasm and creativity!

Add Your Favourite Recipe

Do you have an all-time favourite family recipe that you'd like to share? We'd love to hear from you! Write your recipe here, then take a picture and email it to: *cookbooks@nourishns.ca*